HOW TO
PAY LESS
FOR MORE

HOW TO PAY LESS FOR MORE

THE CONSUMER'S GUIDE TO NEGOTIATING
THE BEST DEALS – WHATEVER YOU'RE BUYING

MARC LOCKLEY

howtobooks

ACKNOWLEDGEMENTS

This book was made possible with the support of Sharon, my very patient and supportive wife. My two sons Luke and Matthew, who continue to sharpen my skills by constantly negotiating extended bed times and more hours on the Playstation!

Negotiation development began in earnest when I observed, at the age of seven, my father successfully haggling with shop owners and my mother hiding in embarrassment at his shameless way of asking for a discount. From that day on, I realised that negotiation paid dividends. Finally, I would like to thank my good friend Steve Cviic, without whose skilful editing and constant motivation whilst reading my transcripts, I think this book would have struggled to get past Chapter 1.

How To Books Ltd
Spring Hill House, Spring Hill Road,
Begbroke, Oxford OX5 1RX, United Kingdom
Tel: (01865) 375794 Fax: (01865) 379162
info@howtobooks.co.uk
www.howtobooks.co.uk

The right of Marc Lockley to be identified as author of this work has been asserted by him in accordance with the Copyright, Design and Patents Act 1988.

British Library Cataloguing in Publication Data
A catalogue record for this book is available from
the British Library.

First published 2008

ISBN: 978 1 84528 237 0

Cover and text illustrations by David Mostyn
Produced for How To Books by Deer Park Productions, Tavistock
Typeset by *specialist* publishing services ltd, Montgomery
Printed and bound by Bell & Bain Ltd, Glasgow

Contents

1
So how are you going to save me thousands?

WHY THE BOOK?

Well, put simply, have you ever felt you were paying too much for things?

Have you ever put something back on the shelf because you didn't agree with the price?

Have you walked away with your purchase feeling that you got a raw deal?

What about being at the shops the next day and seeing the product on sale elsewhere for less?

Also, if you did get a deal, could it have been better?

BUT NEGOTIATION IS FOR PROFESSIONALS ISN'T IT?

No, it's not. Negotiation isn't just for sales people and their business associates. It isn't a skill only learnt in the training rooms of large corporations. It's a skill that is available to everyone who is willing to put in some preparation, think about what they say, know what they want to achieve and understand how to ask for it.

BUT ALL THE LITERATURE ON NEGOTIATION IS AIMED AT THE BUSINESS MARKET

Yes. This book aims to change that, giving the consumer the tools, ideas and mindset to achieve better deals in their life's purchases. It does involve theory (but not too much!), with more of an emphasis on putting your own natural skills into action, and it's written in an easy-to-follow format.

WHAT'S THE POINT OF NEGOTIATING IF IT IS ONLY GOING TO SAVE ME A FEW POUNDS?

It's amazing how a 'few pounds' add up. The table below sets out a few ways in which I have saved money and gained added extras by using the techniques and ideas found in this book.

Item/idea	Full-rate price	Negotiated price	Saving
2 nights in a luxury hotel	£1,500	£750 + chocs and Champagne	£750
Annual mobile contract	£497	£370	£127
Compensation: phone bill	-	-	£30
Internet package+calls	£360	£245 + free phone	£115
Gym membership	£845	£672 + free towels	£173

DVD postal library	£135	£45	£90
Home/content insurance	£350	£320	£30
Total saving	£1,315 + approximately £170 of value		

And, every four or five years, there is a good chance that you will either move, have major work done to the house (for example, a loft extension or new kitchen), or buy a new car.

Item	Full-rate price	Negotiated price	Saving
3-bedroomed house	£110,000	£92,000	£18,000
Loft extension	£35,000	£32,500	£2,500
Wedding	£22,000	£19,650	£2,350
Family car	£15,107	£12,600	£2,507

In fairness, the loft extension and the wedding are not actual amounts that I know have been saved by techniques from this book (as yet) but are merely examples to prove a point. However, both the house and the car are real, personal examples.

So, buying this book could prove to be the best single investment you have ever made.

And learning to negotiate can do more than save you money – it may even help you in your relationships (more about this in the final chapter).

WHERE CAN YOU NEGOTIATE?

It would perhaps be easier to say where you can't negotiate. For example: National Insurance contributions, council tax, and parking fines (though skills you learn in negotiation may help you contest them!). Negotiation happens all around us, from the electrical store to the estate agent.

CAN ANYONE DO IT?

Virtually anyone. If you have the will to do it, and use the chapters as a framework for your negotiation, you will stand every chance of saving money. The main thing is to have the right mindset and not to feel embarrassed by the idea of striking deals.

Eleanor Roosevelt once said: 'No-one can make you feel inferior without your consent'. In negotiation, the rule is: 'No-one can make you feel ripped off without your consent.'

WHY CAN I HELP?

Like most people, I was born with an inner negotiator, which I used even in my cot to demand milk by screaming the house down! However, I later graduated to more persuasive and less drastic techniques, using these to get my first personal stereo for £5 less than the asking price, gain a great discount for a brand new car, and then buy my first house at 15% below the advertised rate. In all instances, both parties were happy with the deal they got; it all came down to skills that I learnt and developed through the years.

My professional negotiating started off with the first advert I sold for £75 with the *Racing Post*. I spent the next 20 years in the UK's national newspaper industry, heading up teams that sold to some of the best advertising talents in the country. By the time I became Head of Agency Sales at the *Daily Mail*, I was regularly negotiating multi-million pound group deals.

In 2005, I gained coaching qualifications from *CoachU*, a world leading organisation, and founded *Lockley Associates*, developing individuals through coaching. I specialise in supporting individuals to help them develop their inner talents to become great negotiators both in business and in life.

This book has been in my mind for over ten years. The skills are not great secrets kept in the vaults of businesses, but they are rarely spoken about, and people have often asked me: 'How did you get such a great deal?'

Frankly, I find negotiation fun. When you get a better deal because of your efforts, it leaves you with a real sense of achievement.

HOW WILL I KNOW WHEN I CAN NEGOTIATE?

When you have successfully got a price lower than that on the tag.

HOW TO USE THIS BOOK

Read this book from cover to cover to create your own strategy for success. Or you can also use it as a quick reference by reading the relevant chapter related to your particular negotiation needs. The ideas are not the only route, or indeed necessarily the right route for you. They are suggestions that you may use as they are, or use to help you to create your own negotiation template.

The book is split into three sections:

Section A: Fundamental elements to negotiating (Chapters 2 and 3)

This is for people who want to develop their inner negotiator. It examines the general process involved, and also the importance of verbal and non-verbal sales techniques, including body language. This section has the added bonus of helping you understand some of the skills used in everyday life to read and understand people.

Section B: Templates for success in consumer negotiations (Chapters 4 to 10)

These chapters will use specific examples where negotiation can make a significant difference in the deals that you encounter. From buying or selling property to your luxury weekend break away, examples and explanations are given, with the aim of saving or making you money. Follow the guidelines to create your own template for success.

Section C: Work-related negotiations (Chapters 11 and 12)

This section is set apart from the rest, as the negotiations here have a significant bearing on long-term relationships and need to be handled accordingly. Working conditions are important to get right, to be able to balance life well; whether that means better pay or more flexible working, it's important that you get the terms that you are happy with. These chapters will look at pay rises and also flexible and part-time hours.

STEALTH TACTICS

Now and again you will see a 'stealth tactic' in the chapters. These are tactics that can find things out or help you negotiate more effectively without the individual being aware what you are doing. They go under the radar, like a Stealth fighter.

Ultimately, this book is about giving you ideas of how to approach businesses and individuals. There are many different approaches and the book is written to highlight some of these, but is by no means the only way for you to get the deal you want.

A NOTE TO BUSINESSES

This book is written to 'facilitate trade' between a consumer and a business. Often, companies miss out on business because people find things too expensive or need to spend their money on other items. However, the potential buyer does not always return to the shop to articulate their objections to the price or package offered.

This book will help the consumer's pound go that much further, and allow you to negotiate terms that will give you their custom.

A NOTE FOR THE CONSUMER

This book is intended to help you get a better deal, thereby saving (or making) you money.

Although it is up to the company whether they take your business, for you as a consumer it is worth remembering that a 'win-win' deal, where both parties come out with something that they want, is often a better solution. This may be particularly relevant when dealing with small businesses, like a small guest-house whose owner may be able to supply good local information and discounted attraction vouchers to a 'great guest'.

SECTION A

FUNDAMENTAL ELEMENTS OF NEGOTIATING

This section of the book will help awaken the negotiator within and make him or her an integral and natural extension of yourself. The information is not exhaustive, but it will give you a logical framework upon which you can base your own experience and observation.

Most of it **is** logical. When I have run coaching sessions on negotiation, in business or personal life, the participants often claim not to know the process, and can't read body language. However, through logic and effective questioning, they are surprised to discover how perceptive their inner negotiator is. This section of the book will help you to realise this and develop your skills to a greater level.

These two chapters are jam-packed with processes, ideas and mindsets that I have learnt during four decades of negotiating both in business and personal life.

2
Practical guide to any negotiation

SO WHAT IS NEGOTIATION?

To me, it is to bargain to reach an agreement – ideally acceptable to both (or all) parties. The harder you negotiate, the more likely it is that you will tip the scales in your favour.

What you need to beware of is pushing so far that the other person doesn't want to play any more. In this case you have failed to create or, indeed, develop any long-term relationship. When trading one-off deals with shops this may not necessarily be a high a priority to you, but you never know when you may return – I will leave that to your judgement.

However, if you can justify what you are offering and make the other person feel happy with their lot (although maybe not skipping out of the room!), then you have not only created an effective deal for yourself, you may also be able to create bigger and better deals in the future. This is especially true when it comes to negotiating in shops or staying in hotels which you regularly visit.

It **is** possible to have a win-win negotiation. You get the price you want and, as an example, a hotel manager sells his room and gains new customers.

But often people feel embarrassed at the very thought of negotiating.

THE EMBARRASSMENT MYTH

In many countries it is deemed rude *not* to negotiate! Bartering is something that is expected and enjoyed in bazaars around the world, and the market traders are the best around. I remember in Turkey being welcomed into a shop, introduced to a fine array of clothing, sat down and treated to a cup of tea whilst two gentleman eagerly punched in various numbers on a calculator, playing good cop, bad cop until eventually I was charmed into buying lovely jackets for myself and my wife, having negotiated down to almost half the asking price. Both parties parted happy with the deal, and I had had a really enjoyable hour (this was close to midnight!)

And in the world of big business, too, negotiation is the rule, rather than the exception. Bear in mind that the corporations you purchase items from have negotiated deals with suppliers to get the products on the shelves in the first place. For example: a cup of coffee, from farm to cup goes through several negotiation stages. The farmer sells to local traders, and then the coffee in its original form goes to a central location before being sent to a cleaning station. The beans will often go to government auction and are then shipped to a roasting company. Then they are packaged, exported and sent to the stores themselves. The price has changed significantly since it has left the farmer (depending upon where you buy the coffee, the farmer usually gets between one and ten percent of the final price sold). Why should the process of negotiation stop there? I am not necessarily suggesting you barter for your mocha cappuccino when you next go to your coffee shop, but you get my drift! The same theory applies to many products.

OK, so you shouldn't be embarrassed about negotiation, but people often think it's a tough thing to do.

THE 'NEGOTIATION IS TOUGH' MYTH

Catching a ball is tough unless you practise. Both negotiation and catching a ball become easier when you give them a go and learn from your experiences. If you make negotiation habitual then you will do it without thinking about it. The beauty of it is that it presents itself to us almost every day, so we have plenty of opportunities to practise.

Is there a process to negotiation?

Yes there is.

Prepare

↓

Discuss

↓

Propose

↓

Bargain

↓

Agree

The five stages of negotiation.

Negotiation courses talk about their own versions of this, and often add in one or two areas for good measure, but to me, this is what it boils down to: a simple five-stage process.

Whether you are in business or not, this works extremely effectively; however, it is also combined with a softer skill that can be nurtured to great effect, and that is how you communicate.

We cover this in the next chapter.

I. PREPARATION

As you read the book you will notice how much emphasis is put on preparation. Preparation can account for up to 70% of a negotiation and affects four out of five of the stages: from understanding what it is you want to buy; researching into the range of prices companies charge; to deciding on a price range that you are happy to pay and on an alternative idea if that price isn't reached. This is the centre of your wheel: without it you are not going to get very far.

Without sufficient preparation, you are relying too heavily on your sales patter, and, if you are exposed, your lack of background information and defined pricing parameters could get you a deal that's not right for you, or worse still, no deal at all. On the other hand, too much information could get you confused. A balance is right: if you feel you are getting too bogged down, cut out the bogged-down bits, and create a crib sheet of information. Clear and concise points that are in logical order will give you all the salient reasons needed to get the price you want.

You need to decide how much time it's worth spending on this. Let's look at negotiation from the perspective of being employed and what hourly rate would be acceptable. For example, if you are only saving £5 on an MP3 player, think of the saving as wages earned: £5 equals, say, 20 minutes' work. However, when it comes to saving money on buying a new car that may save you up to £1,500, it's more likely to be worth spending around three or four days on preparation.

An example crib sheet is detailed at the end of this chapter.

The best way to prepare is to ask yourself the following questions.

Are there any current events that may affect the negotiation?

It's amazing what you can hear on the news, read in the paper or stumble upon on the internet that would indicate the state of a particular market or client. This can be very obvious: for example, a headline stating that some travel agents are dramatically reducing package holiday prices due to the unusually hot weather we are having in our own country, along with the fact that people are embracing 'dynamic packaging' (booking individual elements of their holidays mainly via the internet) will tell you that there are great deals to be had.

There can also be other, less obvious, implications of a news item like this. Hot weather tends to drive people to beaches and parks – and away from the high street. So stores that sell televisions and DVDs, for example, will have less foot-fall, and are more likely to be willing to negotiate on price. But it can work the other way too: it'll be harder to get good deals on barbecues and garden furniture, for example, during the same period of hot weather. So, think about what you are hearing, reading or seeing, and take a view on the impact of this on what you intend to purchase.

What can you find out about the company you are going to negotiate with that will help you get the best deal?

So much information is available on most companies and, again, it depends on how detailed you need or want to be. Company websites are often a good place to start. Would a company prospectus be handy to view before you trade with them? These can often give you information on mission statements, profit and loss, areas of growth, etc.

Have there been any recent special offers that you are aware of? How can you find out?

Being aware that a hotel has recently been doing a three-nights-for-the-price-of-two promotion, or a telecom company has been offering a free internet phone if you subscribe for 18 months, can help. Although that deal may not still be on, you realise that the company is promotion-led, and offering value is part of their strategy. Although the deal is not currently available, why not ask for it anyway, stating you know it was relevant two weeks ago? Many companies create regular offers to entice new customers and just package them up in different ways – one time it may be £10 off and other times a free bottle of wine.

Do you know anyone who has bought from this company before?

Friends or colleagues who have had previous experiences can often help you. For example, your friends Hailey and Luke have recently stayed in a hotel you are thinking of visiting. They noticed at breakfast that there were very few people there and trade was very quiet. This could help you weigh up the likelihood of the hotelier offering you a discount on the advertised rate. Or Amanda had bought a new car and got the navigation system included despite it not being included in the brochure price. These examples make you aware of demand and willingness to trade.

What are their competitors currently offering?

A competitor's deals/offers can influence a company. No-one likes losing business; however, losing it to a rival is even worse, especially if there is a deal that could have been done.

What about the competitors' websites? These can be good to look at for alternative ideas if you didn't reach an agreement with your first choice (an alternative possibility is known as a BATNA: Best Alternative to a Negotiated Agreement).

However, understanding the competition and their offers will also potentially give you the opportunity of negotiating a better rate with your original choice.

For example: purchasing a barbecue in your favourite hardware store.

> 'I do like this barbecue; however, flat4u are offering a similar one with a gas cylinder and an under-tray as well, and it's £10 less. Price is important to me, and if you can beat their price, I am in a position to buy now.'

How keen are they to trade at the moment? How can you find that out?

All of these questions help you calculate the keenness to trade, but is there anything else that could influence this? The more indications you have, the better your chances of gaining a reduction in price or getting added value. For example, a summer sale on its last day – are the retailers wanting to clear all the sale items off the stock so that they can make room for the autumn fashion?

Where can you get all this information?

Today we have a plethora of information-gathering locations. The internet, television, papers, magazines, company sites/prospectuses and speaking to people are six great starting points.

A rapidly growing arena for consumer thoughts can be found in the shape of blogs. A blog is an on-line journal, and there are tens of millions of them. Subjects are varied, and it is highly likely you will find a product you wish to buy being discussed by some happy (and unhappy) purchasers. Plenty of good information can be found from these sites, and can help you to establish the strengths and weaknesses of a potential purchase.

What questions do you want to ask the salesperson?

There may be more you want to know about the product. Will they offer you a discount if you buy two items? What price could they offer if you wanted extras added on? If a competitor offers you a better price, is it worth coming back to see if they will match/beat it? What questions could you ask that will help you get a better deal than the price offered?

Who is the person that will most likely offer me a deal?

More often than not, I would say that this needs to be a decision-maker: for example, the manager or owner. Often, sales assistants will not be able to make discount decisions, and will go and ask the manager on your behalf. In most cases they will just put the bare facts, and not add in the parts that you have tirelessly established during your preparation which will help you gain a better rate. Wherever possible, speak to the person who can influence the deal. In cases where the value being negotiated is high, it may be worth ringing ahead to see if they are in.

Once you have done your research, it may be an idea to write down the key points and read through them, so you have an understanding of information that will help you in your negotiation. If the negotiation is going to be by telephone, then it's easy to have it by your side when you're talking.

2. DISCUSSION

This is where you set out your stall and get the final snippets of information that will help you decide what price you will be happy with.

Whether by phone, face-to-face or by email, this is where you ask your prepared questions. Meeting face-to-face is much better for reading the salesperson, as body language, pace and tonality account for over 90% of the real meaning behind what is being said (see Chapter 3).

When discussing things with the salesperson, have two questions in mind:

'What can I get from this conversation that will help me get a good deal?'

This can include whether you get a discount for volume, for buying with another product, for deciding upon a specific type of wine to go with your wedding meal, or for buying now as opposed to next month.

'What would help them to give me a better deal?'

The second one is important, as 'what's in it for them' certainly helps to get them on your side and potentially more inclined to trade off the full-rate.

Are the shops/showrooms on a specific profit margin on their products?

Profit margins vary, and not all shops work on the same amounts. Some outlets work on a flat percentage profit on all items and are marked up accordingly; at others it varies. Equally, they may have specific products that they need to push and sell and will be incentivised accordingly; this can vary and does not necessarily remain the same week in and week out. Knowing this can help you understand the margins that you may be talking about when negotiating. For example, if all products carry a 10% profit for the store, it's unlikely you would be able to negotiate a discount of 11%. Also, asking where their pressure points are and finding out whether some items/brands have more leverage for negotiation may help you in your quest.

If you get on well with the salesperson and gain rapport (see Chapter 3), then you could be in a better position to ask this sort of question. Understanding 'what's in it for them' can really help you move forward a deal, as, if you match what they want to sell with what you want to buy, then you have more chance to get the offer you want.

Establish their commission structure

Knowing if they are on a bonus system or not can help you understand the salesperson's motivation to trade with you.

3. PROPOSE

This is where business and consumer markets often differ. In the business world, I would usually make the initial proposal, thus allowing me to be in control of the negotiation from the outset. Alongside my proposal, I would also have thought out my rationale as to the price offered and explained this to the customer. From here, the offer might change, as we bargained and I compromised; however, my justifications would remain the same.

But as a consumer, I would probably prefer to hear their offer first, since I could be pleasantly surprised if it is better than the price I might have suggested (though I will give examples of both approaches throughout the book).

Before they propose, though, you need to make a statement that will encourage them to offer you a better deal than the one on the price tag. Preparation again is the key, so ask yourself the question:

> '*What can I say* (given all the information I have found out during my preparation) *that will persuade the salesperson to offer me a great deal?*'

21

This will allow you to be in control of the negotiation without offering a price. The statement needs to have something in it that will catch the attention of the salesperson. Depending on the circumstances, that could be your intention to buy now, in the next day or so, or your offer to buy three or four things if the price is right.

In the case of volume deals, it may be worth lowering their expectations first, and then building on them to gain extra value. For example: start off by saying you are in a position to buy 6 cases of wine, gaining a quote, and then increase the amount of cases if they offer a better price. We will address that in the bargaining part of this chapter.

Even though they will have proposed a price, you should still have several justifications as to why it should be lower. Prepare your justifications beforehand – first stage preparation helps you do this.

One thing to have in mind at the proposal stage is your three outcomes. Again, this is something you can prepare.

Three outcomes

Make sure you think of three outcomes.

Firstly, your **ideal outcome**: a great deal for you, everything you want with all the bells and whistles. However, you need justifiable reasons as to why this price is fair.

Secondly, a **good deal**: OK, you haven't got everything, but you have come out well enough to be happy with the deal you have struck.

Thirdly, the bare minimum: what I call 'the **walk-away rate**'.

Is that the offered price, or do they have to move away from that in order for you to buy? Effective buyers or sellers will often see signs that you will pay the full rate, which is why it is good to understand both the verbal and non-verbal clues that are often given away by both parties (Chapter 3).

Sometimes price is not the only variable, as added extras can help to make a deal great, and it's important to be aware of what else could be included or taken away in order to get the package you want.

Your variables

Apart from price, variables are some things that can be included within a deal, but are not necessarily vital. They are often things that are 'nice-to-have' rather than 'must-haves'.

When it comes to bargaining, these can help to close a deal.

For example, variables when buying a car could be a GPS system, DVD screens in the back for the children, and car mats. Variables when joining a gym could be free towels or additional guest passes.

These are things that you could have already included in your deal or have up your sleeve to add in when the price is not changing. What is important is that you have prepared (there's that word again!) your list beforehand.

4. BARGAINING

This is the haggling stage. This has hopefully already begun, as your opening statement has gained you a better deal than the asking price.

Believe it or not, it may be as simple as asking for a discount and repeatedly saying:

'Oh come on, do it for £150 … What about £160 then?'

and waiting for them to say yes.

Sometimes, I have actually seen this work: when a buyer has looked at someone with puppy dog eyes and begged for a discount, pleading 'Oh, go on'. In a moment of weakness, the off-guard salesperson has crumbled under the strain of such emotional appeal, and knocked off a few pounds, as they feel that saying no would be akin to Scrooge denying Tiny Tim that wholesome meal he so desperately needed in *A Christmas Carol*.

However, as this only has a limited effect, saving the odd pound rather than significant amounts (which is the intention of this book), let's assume that a more considered approach is needed.

The question you need to ask yourself at this stage is:

'What more can I do or offer to influence this deal?'

You have three outcomes and your variables. These, combined with knowing 'what's in it for them', give you all the information you need to negotiate a deal. As a reminder, 'what's in it for them' includes their motivation to negotiate: this was discussed in the preparation stage of this chapter and includes benefits both to the individual salesperson and the company.

The value of 'if and then'

Asking an 'if and then' question is often a valuable negotiation tool in business and in life.

Taking into consideration your outcomes, variables and 'what's in it for them?' an example might be:

> *'I can always do with extra wine if we don't use it for the party. If you let me pay £60 per case then I will buy ten cases instead of six, giving you £600 instead of £360 – nearly 70% more'*

This is known as a conditional offer. The amount of money offered is only applicable if the wine seller accepts the specific deal. If they do, then great; if not, another offer can be suggested.

Do not be afraid to change your variables when taking into consideration the salesperson's response. For example: if you initially put a £300 GPS system into your proposal to buy a new car, but the salesperson suggests a slightly cheaper model to incorporate your suggestion, you can always try and change the variable to make sure you still get the car you want – for example, by asking for car mats and a tank of petrol instead of the GPS.

Bargaining can have several rounds to it, so it's important to begin with your ideal outcome and come down from there if necessary.

5. AGREE

This should be the quickest stage. What is worth doing is summarising the agreement, preferably in writing (unless of course you are buying the product immediately). This avoids any unnecessary misunderstandings.

Equally, if you are unsure about whether they have agreed to your terms, it is good to ask one of two types of questions.

1. **A pre-close question**: this is when you ask them something trivial that will establish whether a deal has been done. For example:

   'That's great. Do you offer a free packaging service?'

   'OK. Can the membership start tonight as I see you have a Pilates class at 7?'

If you are still unsure ...

2. **An assumptive close**: this is when you ask a question that assumes a deal has been done. For example:

   'Who do I make the cheque payable to?'

   'Do you accept Visa?'

If you get the right answers to these, you are aware that the deal has been done.

If the above does not work, it is likely that you have not agreed and you may need to go back to the bargaining area to see if any adjustments need to be made.

An example crib sheet for buying a new computer.	
Must-have	Like-to-have
Notebook/laptop	DVD re-writer
Minimum 15 inch screen	17 inch screen
1-year service	2-year service
Cost under £675	Cost under £600

Wifi capability	TV capability
CD player	Free pack of blank DVDs, CD RWs
0% finance	Free desktop publishing software
Windows Vista Home Premium	Windows Vista Ultimate

Companies and their offers.

	Make/Model	Retailer	Price
Choice 1	Iwantthatone MX5 11	Comps Are Us	£649.99
Has all must-haves, plus DVD RW			
17 inch screen			
Desktop publishing software (DTS), TV capability			
Fast processor and looks flash			
2-yr service. Windows Vista Ultimate			
Choice 2	TMX Mark 2	Direct	£675
All must-haves, plus DVD RW and DTS			
17 inch screen. Windows Vista Ultimate			
2-yr service. Bulky but comes with case			

Choice 3	Pixelpower 7	Digital Dealers	£699.99
All must-haves, plus DVD RW, DTS			
2-yr service			
Great colour and lightweight			

Information on companies
Comps Are Us – advertised in national press 0% interest for 2 years, and blank DVD's reduced from £12.99 to £7.99 this week. Iwantthatone MX5 11 being sold through their major competitors for £675 but includes a laptop bag (maybe see which will do the better deal and offer them my business). Comps Are Us have a store five minutes away from home and therefore easy to go back to if a problem (TMX Mark2 has to be sent back by post and Digital Dealers are an hour away). Weather hot at the moment and stores may be quiet.
[Write similar information for the other companies.]

Information on computers
Blogs have rated Iwantthatone as a great product, however battery life is poor. I am mainly going to use it on the mains, so not a problem to me but I will highlight this negative to the shop.
[Write similar information on your other choices of computer.]

Questions potentially to ask Comps Are Us
'Do you price-match with your local competitors?'
'Having researched the market, I have whittled it down to three computers, one of which you sell; however, price-wise your computer is £100 more than I would ideally spend. If you were to offer it to me for £550 and include a laptop bag, which your competitors do, then I would buy the computer now.'
'If I were to get an offer from another company of £599 for the same product, would you beat it?'

3 outcomes for Iwantthatone
Ideal – £550 with laptop bag

Good – £599 with DVDs
Acceptable – £650 with laptop bag
Based on the above prices I would be happy to buy Iwantthatone.

Best Alternative
(i.e. If I can't reach an agreement within the price ranges above)
TMX Mark 2 if they do it for £640 or below.

Next Action	
By 8th April	Speak to Digital Dealers and discuss with them best price they will offer, as I am keen on three products and price will sway me.
By 10th April	Speak to dealers on TMX Mark 2, get them to offer best price – highlighting new deal offered by Digital Dealers.
By 12th April	Go to Comps Are Us and discuss with them my options and let them know price on TMX Mark 2.

READ ON!

This has hopefully given you a good understanding of the process of negotiation. Like catching a ball, it will only become a natural skill if you put it into practice.

Also, a good proportion of negotiation is decided upon not just by process, but how you communicate with the salespeople, and the next chapter will help you with this.

IN SUMMARY

1. Enjoy the prospect of negotiation. Companies and suppliers have built-in profit margins and are

unlikely to sell to you at a loss. Share the spoils and reap the benefits!

2. The more you do it, the easier it becomes. Make negotiation a habit and it becomes easier over time – especially when you see the financial benefits.

3. Negotiation is a five-stage process: prepare, discuss, propose, bargain and agree. Paying full-rate is two-stage: discuss and agree. The difference between the two is huge!

4. Preparation accounts for up to 70% of the negotiation. It affects four out of five of the stages. Spend an appropriate amount of time, relative to potential savings, on preparation.

5. The discussion phase allows you to fact-find about the likelihood of getting a deal, by asking questions and listening carefully to the answers.

6. Prepare your proposal (or response to a proposal). Have three outcomes in mind: ideal, good and walk-away.

7. 'If and then' is a fantastic bargaining tool.

3
The language of negotiation

INTRODUCTION

The language of negotiation consists of several things: there's what you say; there's how you say it; and there's the way in which manner and body language affect the message you are giving or receiving.

Much of it is common sense, and we don't want to overcomplicate what should, in the end, be a natural process. However, you will hopefully find the technical aspects discussed in this chapter interesting and useful.

First of all, we're going to look at non-verbal communication: body language, pace and tonality. This is useful within negotiation, as it can help you interpret a salesperson's willingness to trade. You can also help determine how you are being perceived, by being aware of your body language.

Secondly, we discuss the use and benefits of rapport. This is also a hugely useful negotiation skill, as the salesperson or buyer is much more likely to work hard to help you if you are getting on with them.

Finally, we look at what you say – the words used in

negotiation. This includes using your words to good effect, or listening out for what your opposite number is saying (or not saying). This last point has a significant impact: we often assume something from what is said – and it isn't always true. As Mark Twain put it: 'What gets us into trouble is not what we don't know, it's what we know for sure that just ain't so.'

I. NON-VERBAL COMMUNICATION

It may come as a surprise to you to learn how much of the power of any verbal message comes down to the **way** in which it is said, and the gestures that accompany it. If you take, for example, the simple phrase, 'That's great!', what is your initial thought? What is being conveyed?

It may depend on the mood you are in. Do you think:

a. It's a positive and excited response to receiving some good news? For example, someone has just won the jackpot in the lottery (though I imagine, in that case, that there might be a few more unprintable words involved as well!).

b. Or is it a sarcastic answer to news that someone is annoyed at? For example, they have bought 50 lottery tickets without winning a bean!

In so far as these things are measurable, it's been estimated that the actual words used account for less than 10% of the meaning behind a message – the rest is conveyed by pace, tone and body language. And that is why in this book I often say that where possible you should buy products face-to-face (assuming that it beats the internet package on offer).

If you can't negotiate face-to-face, the telephone is better than email or letter, but although it is then possible to hear the words used and interpret the tonality, you cannot pick up on body language – which accounts for so much.

So what is body language?

Body language is communication through postures, expressions and gestures (encompassing the whole body, including the face). Often these are unconscious movements, although senior politicians – amongst others – are taught to communicate effectively in this way.

The beauty of body language (and, in fact, negotiation) is that you have opportunities to practise, observe and learn every day. Key give-away areas are: the eyes, the mouth, the arms, the legs, the hands and posture. From these, many moods and emotions can be read to allow you to understand whether or not someone is ready to buy, sell, or agree to your terms.

Six basic emotions

There are many different opinions on which are the true basic human emotions; however, I'm going to take six that I believe are fundamental.

happiness   sadness   fear

From these basic emotions, others come. For example, within the context of negotiation, happiness is similar to interest – if a salesperson is looking happy as he talks to you, he is likely to be interested in doing a deal (this is not rocket science!).

So why is it important to understand body language?

Would you rather pay £10,000 less for your next property, simply because you have realised from the seller's manner that he/she is anxious/eager to sell?

When buying a car, although you have already negotiated a GPS system, wouldn't it be great if you could also get a better CD player and a full tank of petrol for no extra cost? And all because you saw that the salesperson was nodding and smiling when you asked for the GPS system to be included!

Understanding body language, and reacting effectively to it, can help you get more from a deal – it can also help you realise when it's time to stop, as you have got all that you can.

Reading body language

In the table below are some signs that may help you interpret how the negotiation is faring. Remember to take things in context, and wherever possible look for two or three signs, rather than one.

Body Language	Possible interpretation
Nodding positively Smiling Good eye contact Licking of lips Open stance (arms and legs not crossed – though be aware some people merely find this comfortable) Leaning forward/strong posture Rolling up sleeves (unless they are getting physical!)	Showing interest. You may have already asked for the CD player in the car, why not then add another item whilst you are on a roll, for example, metallic paint or alloy wheels (or even both)?
Slightly scrunched eyes Stroking chin Hand to cheek Making noises like 'mmmm'	Making a decision. If they do a lot of this and say no – perhaps you're agonisingly close to them agreeing a deal.
Looking away Tugging ear Rubbing eyes Running fingers through their hair Slouched posture	Not interested. Establish if this is the case and what could make them interested: for example, is it price or the timing of your purchase?
Looking away (perhaps towards where the decision-maker is) Showing indecision Slouched posture Fidgeting	Not a decision-maker (in which case, politely find out who is). You need to speak to someone who has the authority to package a better deal.

Rubbing nose (or it could be they just have an itch!)	Expressing doubt in your story (or their own one is not entirely true and they are hiding something)
Looking up and to the right when responding to you	Being creative/telling a lie

The list is by no means exhaustive. Observe people as you interact with them, and build up your own personal portfolio of signs. And remember: awareness of others is key to becoming a good negotiator.

Using the right body language

Unless you are well practised, you should allow your own body language to be natural. It is, however, worth spending some time on how you want to be perceived by your opposite number when you are about to negotiate.

This depends on what you want to achieve. In some situations, you want them to believe that you know what you are doing and won't be messed with. In others, you may want to create the impression that you are wide-eyed and innocent – not a great negotiator, determined to get the best deal you can.

In the main, I aim to come across as somewhere in between: confident, polite, willing to learn and listen, and ready to let them have my money if they treat me fairly.

Getting the best from a salesperson

Often the best way to approach salespeople is realising how they best react to you. Remember the old adage that people buy people, and although the job of a salesperson is to get to know you and your needs, if you can get to know them better, talk to them in a way they understand and establish *their* needs, then you will probably generate the best from them, and that could mean a better deal for you. This is often referred to as gaining rapport.

2. RAPPORT

What is rapport?

Rapport is when you create mutual trust and respect and instinctively begin to interact effortlessly with someone. Rapport is likely to be most successful when it is genuine and not fabricated; this is why it is important to have a real interest in the people you are dealing with. The best salespeople out there are masters at gaining rapid rapport with people. When you know, like and trust someone you are much more likely to be able to negotiate with them to best effect. Of course, there are also slimy salespeople who try to appear to be your best friend when clearly they're not – we all know how genuinely that comes across! There are several ways to gain rapport, and you are best advised to pick one that suits your personality and style, as it will come over more genuinely than if you look as though you are following a process you don't totally buy into.

Some ways in which you can gain rapport

1. **The personal touch.** It's highly likely the salesperson will tell you who they are. If they don't, introduce yourself and ask them their name. This makes the conversation much more personal.

2. **Treat people as you would like to be treated.** Salespeople

have to deal with all types of customers: happy ones, sad ones, miserable ones, aggressive ones – and it makes a change when they meet someone who shows a degree of interest, listens, asks questions and appreciates their help. You are much more likely to find things out and weigh up the likelihood of a deal being offered if you do this. Showing genuine interest will get them to reveal more, and also buy into you as a person. Of course, this has to be balanced with not overdoing it and showing too much enthusiasm and keenness, as this can give away the desire for you to buy the product regardless of a discount!

3. **Respect their language.** What is the background of the salesperson? What age group are they? What kind of language are they using? This is not to be stereotypical, but reacting well to the language that they use is an important element of gaining rapport. If they are older, softly spoken and obviously from a middle class background, they will respond more effectively if you can (genuinely) speak to them in a similar way, rather than saying: 'All right, my son, how's it going? Can you give me the low-down on this freezer, geezer?' However, if they are young, trendy and quite laid back, a more matey approach may be appropriate, if, and only if, you don't look like a complete berk trying to emulate them! If you are too far removed from their language, then just be yourself without your more extreme ways and remember the first two points.

4. **Maintain good eye contact.** Eye contact has many uses. It shows interest, genuineness, confidence, and allows you to observe the other person from a body language point of view, giving you vital clues as to their intentions to trade and authenticity. Wearing sunglasses whilst talking to a salesperson is putting a barrier between you and them,

so unless the sun is shining brightly in your eyes, put them away!

5. **Choose the right person to do the deal.** Experience has shown that sometimes it may be worth considering someone else to do the talking. Although I am an experienced negotiator, my wife has often had more success than I in getting what **we** want. If it means an added £30 off, then it's worth swallowing your pride and allowing someone else to do the deal. The beauty of negotiating in shops is that you can try and use your persuasion, and then, if you feel you could have struck a better deal, ask your friend or partner to go in ten minutes later and have a try (unless, of course, there is only one item left in stock and there is every likelihood it will go within that time).

3. VERBAL COMMUNICATION

The importance of what is said

A. What you say
An important element of keeping a negotiation going is to make sure you do not give away strong buying signals (see Glossary). Now, of course it is obvious that you have interest in a product; otherwise you wouldn't be in the shop asking about it. However, as long as the salesperson believes that you have options, and you are not committed to their product, then you are keeping the door open and maintaining their keenness to trade with you.

Using phrases like:

*'I am **thinking** of buying an MP3 player and there are*

*a number of **options** I am **considering**, including the
ZX322, CT26i, Radians LT123.'*

Is infinitely better than saying:

*'I **love** the CT26i that has a **whopping** 20GB and the
amazing sound that comes from the speakers.'*

The words in bold in the first example create an impression of
choice: in other words, 'I might buy, but I'm not committed to
the make.'

The words in bold in the second example are pound signs in
the salesperson's eyes!

If you are in a position to buy that day, make sure the
salesperson knows that, as this will probably gain you more
attention and you will be taken seriously. This is especially the
case when the product price is high, for example with a car.

It is also worth using language that will keep the salesperson
on their toes. For example, by ensuring they realise that price
or a better package is what will determine who gets your
business, without it sounding arrogant or rude. At the end of
the day most people have pride, and if they feel you are
pushing things too far, they may decide losing business is less
bad than selling their soul for a quick buck.

Here is an example of how to phrase things politely:

*'I realise the advertised offer is £299.99; however, the
important thing to me is that I get a good price. I feel
that I might get a better offer if I shop around [list the
places if you have them and they ask]. I am in a position
to buy now, if I feel that I have got value. Is there
anything you can do to help me?'*

Here, no demands are made and you have empowered them to make a decision by asking for their help.

B. What they say

Listening out for what they say may help you to get a better deal. When a salesperson pushes (a sales term for selling a specific product or service) a particular model or make, it could be for two reasons. Firstly, they have listened to your requirements, and, with their product knowledge, have matched this with a particular make or model. Secondly, it could be that the store has been told to promote this make or model, and the salesperson has his 'company hat' on. If it's the second reason, you may have more room to be able to strike a better deal.

Another idea would be to simply enquire;

'How's business today/this week/at the moment?'

Or

'What products would you recommend?'

… and listen out for their answers. If business is quiet or even consistent, then perhaps there is more likelihood that they will be willing to offer you a deal. If they say that 'it's hectic at the moment' and they are rushed off their feet, then maybe it will prove more difficult. Though if they say this and you are the only one in the store, you may want to debate the genuineness of the answer to your question!

The importance of what is NOT said

What is not said is often as, or more important than, what is actually said.

A. What you don't say

Good salespeople are trained to recognise this. For example, if you say '£500 is too expensive for this', then the negotiation begins – you have raised an objection: in this case, price. What the statement implies is, 'I am interested, but not at £500.' So if you are happy to buy, but don't want to pay that price, you may want to try offering that as an objection:

'I quite like the product, but £500 is too expensive.'

… and wait for a response. Or if you think you don't want to leave anything to chance, add:

'If you reduce the price [or add in an item you would like for free], *then I may be interested.'*

STEALTH TACTIC What you don't say is often a great tool to use yourself when you are selling, for example, your property or your car. For example, mentioning that another couple are coming for their second (or third) viewing tomorrow makes people think that the property could be sold tomorrow, and, if interested, they should consider making an offer immediately.

B. What they don't say

Always think of this when a salesperson is speaking to you. Do not assume anything. Good salespeople will never lie, but if they leave you with an idea which encourages you to purchase, but which is not strictly true, then it's not in their interest to correct you. For example:

'Well madam, the XTCi HD TV is literally flying off the shelves.'

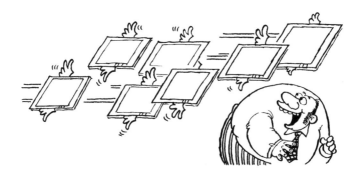

What the salesperson is **not** saying is: 'we have run out'. It may be the case that they have sold 20, but still have ten in stock and their standard stock delivery in a day's time will deliver a further 20. However, the impression is: 'limited availability – buy now!'

'Never **assume** anything: 'it makes an **ASS** out of **U** and **ME**' is a great phrase to remember. Make sure you clarify:

'How many have you got in stock at the moment?'

If they say 'Errr ten', then let the negotiation begin.

IN SUMMARY

1. There are two ways that we communicate: verbally and non-verbally.

2. Listen to and observe the person you are negotiating with. Body language, pace and tonality account for over 90% of the real meaning behind a message, compared with the actual words used, which account for less than 10%.

3. Draw up your own list of visual and verbal signs that people give away and use them to help you interpret people's thoughts. Remember, when possible, not to rely on just one sign.

4. When analysing your own body language, try to give off the impression you want to create. Often this is best when you are confident, polite, interested and you are there to buy if the price is right!

5. People buy people. Where relevant, refer to them by name, listen attentively and ask questions. Speak to them in a tone and language that they relate to – this can be observed quite quickly by listening to them talking to somebody else.

6. Listen for what is said and also what is **not** said, and analyse the real meaning in the context of the negotiation.

SECTION B

TEMPLATES FOR SUCCESS IN CONSUMER NEGOTIATIONS

Well, you've either skipped straight to the epicentre of the book to get on with something specific, or you've read the first few chapters, kind of got it, but need some more specific tips to help you make or save lots of money.

The following seven chapters are dedicated to specific types of negotiations. They are some of the main ones I think will come up, but I am sure you will have your own opinion on that.

Products and prices are fictitious and should not be used (and especially not shown!) to salespeople with the words: 'Well, the expert says I can buy it at this, and he must be right!'

Remember that the end result is to get a good deal. In order to do this, you should mirror the behaviour of what I would deem a good salesperson: be polite, friendly, confident, and make your opposite number feel at ease; show interest and, above all, keep your wits about you!

4
Buying a property

Buying a property is likely to be the single biggest personal investment you ever make. Getting the right place is obviously paramount, but so is getting it for the right price.

In recent years, this has been a challenging market and it is easy to feel daunted when entering it. However, I believe this is unnecessary, as house prices are often negotiable, and it is always perfectly possible to get good deals. My only word of warning would be that you should recognise how much emotion is involved when choosing a property. And the more emotionally attached you are to a place, the harder it is to negotiate, as the stakes are higher than mere bricks and mortar. So, decide in your own mind whether you are prepared to negotiate and potentially lose out, if the deal is not right for you.

The demand for property will fluctuate and also plays a part in how much you can bargain. You can of course leave it up to the estate agent, but taking control of your own negotiation can have its advantages – not least the fact that emotionally and financially it is in your interests to get the price you want. You can either decide to negotiate the property personally, direct with the sellers (that is assuming they are happy with this), or 'manage' the estate agent, giving them instructions on how to pursue your purchase.

If you decide to do a private purchase, then this has its advantages for both parties, as there is no commission to be paid to an estate agent. There are plenty of websites that will give you advice on how to go about this.

Whichever route you decide to take, this chapter will allow you to plan the purchase of your property, understand what will help you calculate any potential movements in price, and be armed with ideas of what you could add into the deal before you agree.

SETTING THE SCENE

You are walking around a three-bedroom semi-detached house, with an estate agent by your side.

> You: *'Well, I have to say this is the only house we've seen that fits the bill. If we are to complete on our own property, and accept the offer, we are going to have to sort this out quickly.'*

> Your partner: *'I agree. Look at the size of this room; my chest of drawers will fit nicely into that corner. Bagsey I sleep by the window!'*

> You: *'I wonder if they would sell us the curtains – what do you think, Graham?'*

> Graham, the estate agent: *'I'll ask Mrs Askew, but I know they really like them and wanted to take them with them.'*

> You: *'Do you think the asking price is negotiable?'*

> Graham: *'It's a really sought after property and area,*

and we have had two couples come back for a second viewing already today. I suggest you get your offer in now before anyone else does.'

You: *'What do you think, darling?*

Your partner: *'I love it and we need to complete soon, otherwise we are in danger of losing the offer on our house.'*

Assessing the above

1. Beware of appearing too keen, whether in front of the estate agent or indeed the sellers. Telling them it ideally 'fits the bill' is like saying 'where do you want me to sign?' Remain interested, but not totally committed. It's obvious when you make an offer that you are keen, as you wouldn't fork out hundreds of thousands of pounds on something you were indifferent about.

2. Don't back yourself into a corner. Showing that you have to buy quickly (in this case your own sale will fall through if you don't purchase soon) is like flashing pound signs to the seller. It can come over as if you are much more likely to extend your offer to your limits in order to do a deal. Again, keep this information to yourself as much as possible, or say that you are happy, if it suits the sellers, for a quick sale.

3. Designing your room in front of the sellers is giving away vital clues. Openly creating your image of beauty will let them believe you are very keen and therefore much more likely to pay the asking price.

4. Why buy the curtains if they could be included in the price? Curtains, wardrobes, carpets and kitchen units can be very

valuable to you when you purchase a property, saving you hundreds of pounds when you could do with the money in your pocket. However, these are often of significantly less value to the seller as they may not fit nicely into their new property. Hold back on fixtures and fittings until you are into the negotiation.

5. What salesmen don't say is often as important as what they do say. When you asked Graham whether the price was negotiable, what he didn't say was 'no'. He answered it with a statement about the property being sought after. You can always ask the question again, to get a 'yes or no' answer. In fairness, the answer could be 'possibly'!

THE BENEFITS OF NEGOTIATING

1. Gaining a better price for the house you want to buy and possibly saving you tens of thousands of pounds. If you are selling a property as well, make sure you read the next chapter.

2. If you decide to 'go it alone' and buy privately, then you and the sellers could save the estate agency commission. Estate agents usually take a percentage of the final sale (percentages vary) and this adds up to thousands of pounds. If a seller is deciding to sell privately, then you should also be able to benefit from this.

3. Potentially valuable added extras: curtains, carpets, wardrobes, etc.

4. As part of the deal, arrange permission to measure up the property before you complete.

FINDING THE RIGHT PLACE — PREPARATION

List what's important to you in a home; what is a must-have and a nice-to-have.

Must-have	Nice-to-have
• pay no more than £290,000 (ideally £275,000) • minimum 3 bedrooms • 2 bathrooms • large kitchen • close to children's school (10 minutes' walk max.) • big garden or park within 10 minutes' walk	• off-street parking • semi-detached • loft extension • separate study • en-suite bathroom with main bedroom • all fixtures and fittings included in the price

LOOKING AROUND

It is easy to fall in love with a property and convince yourself it must be the place to buy; however, often, if you look around there are a few other places that may fit your criteria, and aesthetic changes could bring them up to the standards you want.

Another benefit of looking around is that it will help you establish the price range that is available. If for example, the three-bedroom, two-bathroom property you desire is £295,000, but a similar one down the road is on the market for £275,000, you may be able to use this information as a bargaining tool.

Once you have explored the market, cross check your potential properties with your list of criteria and list them in preference order.

THE CONVERSATIONS WITH AN ESTATE AGENT

It's important to remember that estate agents are business people, and with this in mind, it's worth thinking about what they are trying to achieve. They vary in their approach; however, they earn money from the sale of a property, not to have it on their books for months on end, only earning commission/bonus when the deal goes through. They are profesional salespeople and will listen out for buying signals that you offer; they will also 'sell' the virtues of the house and its surrounds, and are not paid to point out the pitfalls.

However, they are not normally used to skilled negotiators dealing with them in the residential market, so use what you want from the tips below.

WHEN SEEING THE PROPERTY FOR THE FIRST TIME

1. Begin with the end result in mind. You want to buy your property at a good price. Make sure the estate agent/seller is aware you are looking at several houses or flats that suit your needs and desires, and that this property falls into that category. This will assure them that you are serious about potentially purchasing, but are prepared to keep your options open and are not relying on one house in particular.

2. Show interest, but don't give away those buying signals! (See Glossary and Chapter 3.) As we said earlier, avoid letting them know that you are certainly intending to buy by measuring up and 'visualising' how things will look. These are just two signs that are potential give-aways. Others include how you would change the garden; working out how

quickly you would get to work compared with your previous location; the schools being so much better and whether you stand a chance of getting your children into them.

STEALTH TACTIC Highlight the pros and cons of the property in your discussions. For example: 'Your house is really well kept. I like the size of the rooms, but was hoping for a slightly larger dining room.' This pays the seller a compliment, making them feel positive towards you. The statement also highlights a positive point to the house, as well as a negative, and can leave the impression that you are interested but not fully convinced.

STEALTH TACTIC Ask a few questions you know the answers to where the answer is negative. For example: 'How far are the local schools?' You know that the nearest is five miles away, which seems a big distance, but you drive past it every day to get to work. Again, people don't like giving negative answers when they are trying to sell something, and it can leave the impression that they have some work to do for you to buy the property. In the case where they have lots of interest, this may not work; however, if they are keen to sell quickly or have few serious viewers, it may help to get them to reduce the asking price.

3. Keep in mind that the owners could still be emotionally attached to their home. This can make a difference. If people are faced with the choice of selling it to someone who reassures them that their home is going to a good couple/family who will love it and look after it, compared with an indifferent lot, they are much more likely to want the former, and could sell to you at a lower price. Certainly, at the very least, if they have two identical offers, it is highly likely they will sell to the people they like more.

4. Chat to the owner/estate agent and fact-find. Gaining rapport (see Chapter 3) can really help you to find out useful information. See the list below for a few examples.

Be careful to make sure it doesn't sound like an interrogation! Allow time between questions.

'It's a lovely area, are you just upgrading to a bigger house?' *'Where are you moving to?'* *'Have you found a place to stay?'* *'Are you moving with work?'* *'What do you do?'*	These questions could help you to find out whether the move is needed quickly or not. Urgency is a big factor in price. It also shows that you are interested (beware of going too far and sounding nosey!).
You: *'It's a nice area, are you just upgrading to a bigger house?'* Seller: *'Yes, we are getting married and moving in together.'* You: *'Congratulations! When's the big day?'* Seller: *'In three months' time.'* You: *'Have you found a place to live?'* Seller: *'Yes, a 3-bed house, on the other side of town.'*	Again, this indicates that the sellers are happy with a property and the wedding is not that far away. We know how hard they can be to plan (see Chapter 7).

Example conversations that help you find out information such as the need to sell quickly.

OFFERING A PRICE

Now you have had a good look around, you can whittle down your list to perhaps two or three places. Alternatively, there may be just one property you are interested in – if the price is right. In either case, read on …

1. Have in mind how much you are willing to pay. Think of the maximum you are prepared to go to and also your opening offer (which, if you are negotiating, should be lower than your maximum). Could you pay more if they throw in the fixtures and fittings (carpets, wardrobes, curtains, etc.)? If you have more than one property to choose from, do this exercise for all of them.

2. In the case of you only offering a price on one property, think of what you are going to say to the estate agent or seller about the reason for your offer. For example, 'I would like to make an offer of £275,000 (advertised price of £295,000). The good news is I have a confirmed offer on my current house and I am prepared to go ahead now if you agree on the price.' Or alternatively: 'I am prepared to offer the asking price if all the fixtures and fittings are included.' Both these statements make your offer conditional, i.e. you are prepared to pay this rate **if** they agree to your terms.

3. If you have more than one property in mind, call them all. It is a personal choice which you approach first; however, let's assume you start by calling your second choice (out of two). You can sound them out in terms of interest to negotiate. See below for an example conversation. Remember to prepare beforehand what you are going to say, using relevant information that you have already gathered, including your market knowledge and awareness of how keen the sellers are to complete quickly. This ensures that you gain maximum impact with the seller/estate agent.

'Hi Melanie. I have given your property serious thought, and to be honest it's down to two choices, and yours is one of them. If I were to offer you £275,000, would you accept? There are no guarantees, but I will give you a straight yes or no within 24 hours.'	'Well Dave, we will still keep it on the market, but if no-one makes an offer between now and then, I will accept £280,000. Can you let me know as soon as possible?'

An example of a sounding out offer. No guarantees by either party, but a genuine offer if the conditions are met.

'Hi Geoff. We have whittled down our choice to two houses which we like equally; it's now down to price. We have a buyer for our existing property who wants to sign the deal right away. If you agree to £275,000 now, then we will agree and call our solicitors immediately.'	'OK Dave, I am happy to go to £280,000 but that's as low as we can go.'

An example of a 'conditional offer' whereby you are only committed if they agree to your terms.

An example of moving ahead with the above conversation would be as shown on the next page.

The example below also shows how 'trading variables' (see Glossary) can help you agree a deal. In this case, Dave decided that he could afford the asking price and would be happy to buy immediately (subject to survey of course!) **if** the seller would include all the fixtures and fittings (this was included in the 'like-to-have' list at the beginning of the chapter). This is a great example of adding in those final touches that can be so valuable in an overall deal (in this case around £5,000).

Dave: *'That's too much for the house itself, however if you include the carpets, curtains, wardrobes, kitchen and bathroom units, I will be able to meet your asking price as I have budgeted £5,000 for these items. Also I will get the solicitors on to it straight away.'*	Dave is thinking: I know from our previous conversations that they are moving abroad and have no need for these items.
Geoff (seller): *'OK Dave, you hard bargainer! You have a deal!'*	Geoff is thinking: We are moving abroad. We could sell them at auction; however, we need to move quickly and this suits our needs.

An example of bargaining using information previously gained from visiting the house. Both parties gain what they wanted. This is known as a 'win-win' deal.

You may also want to negotiate other things. For example: the completion date, or days for you to go over and 'measure up' curtains, etc. This is always best done prior to closing the deal and can be incorporated into your conditional offer.

'If you agree to exchanging by May 22 and completing on June 1, then I will meet your asking price.'

ALWAYS HAVE IT IN WRITING

Once the deal has been struck, ask for an understanding of the agreement to be sent to you, including all that has been agreed. If a 'for sale' sign has been put up, make sure this is taken down and a 'sold' sign replaces it (or, better still, no sign at all!).

If you wanted to absolutely confirm that all is completed, why not ask a friend to check whether any properties in 'that road' are on the market and see if the one you just bought is still being promoted?

BUYING PRIVATELY – BEFORE THE PROPERTY HITS THE MARKET

Sometimes there is an advantage in buying privately. Firstly, if the market is strong, houses often 'fly off the shelves' and go the same day they hit the market. Secondly, it saves the seller estate agents' fees, and this can help in gaining a better price. More on this in Chapter 5.

A property with a board outside the house already has the sellers committed to the estate agent. However, a good way to find a property not on the market involves a little bit of work. Be creative and think how you can attract people who are thinking of selling but haven't yet started the process.

Here are a few ideas:

1. Create a leaflet that you can put through the letterbox of houses you would consider.

> ## Your house looks great from the outside!
>
> If you are thinking of moving, we are private buyers and want to move to this area and buy a 3-bedroom property.
>
> If you, or someone you know in this area, is thinking of moving, then please call Steve on 01234 5678.

Maybe even find out how much houses are selling for in their road – the more work you do for some people and 'sell' them the idea of the benefits of talking to you, the better your chances.

2. Advertise in the area's local newspaper for a property. This obviously begins to involve cost.

3. Put an advert in the local shop window, being specific about the type of property you would like to buy.

> ## Sell your property and gain an extra £5,000
>
> We are private buyers who wish to buy a 3 bedroom/2 bathroom house in the Boscombe area.
>
> If you are thinking of moving, and would like to save on seller's fees, then please call Steve on 01234 5678.

4. Ask friends in the area to which you want to move, to get in touch with you if they know or hear of anyone thinking of moving.

IN SUMMARY

1. Detail your must-haves and nice-to-haves in a property, and focus your attention on homes that fulfil the criteria.

2. Research the price range of such properties – you may be able to use this to your advantage in the negotiation.

3. If and when you are briefing estate agents, or indeed speaking to the owners of the property you

are viewing, make sure you do not give too many 'buying signals' away.

4. When viewing the property, keep positive about it if you are interested, but still highlight some negatives to keep them guessing (be sure to word the negatives sensitively).

5. Respect the owners' property when viewing it, especially if they are present, and pay them compliments. If people feel that you will look after their house and be good neighbours once you move in, it could tip the balance in your favour.

6. Have some questions to ask the owner/estate agent that may help you find out how quickly the sellers need to sell.

7. When negotiating price, have at least two in mind: your opening offer (the ideal price you would pay and what you would want included for that); and your walk-away rate.

8. Prepare your opening statement to the estate agent/owner to justify your offer.

9. When wanting to make an offer that is based upon certain conditions, use the 'if and then …' technique.

10. Get the agreed offer in writing, including any additional extras that have been included.

5
Selling a property

As a consumer, selling a property is likely to be the largest sum of money that you will be trading with, even if in most cases, the money will be transferred straight to another house or flat. Although you may want assistance from a professional, it's wise to keep close contact with the deal. You have the largest vested interest both financially and emotionally, and it's important to stay in control of all aspects of the sale, including the negotiation. Use this chapter as a guideline to develop your own personal plan for the sale of your property.

DO YOU SELL PRIVATELY OR THROUGH AN ESTATE AGENT?

This book is about negotiation techniques, not general advice-giving, and the choice of whether to sell privately or go through an estate agent is a personal one. Whichever you choose, the important thing is that you have a big influence on the deal. Where else would you allow hundreds of thousands of pounds that belong to you, to be completely in the hands of a stranger? If you go through an estate agent, then take control of what you feel comfortable with, and make sure you let them know clearly what influence you want from the outset. With increased competition (i.e. more estate agents and on-line offerings), lower commission rates can be had, and it's worth shopping around to see the best deals that you can get.

A private sale gives you additional money, as you will not have to pay agency commission. More houses than ever are being sold in this way, and details of how to do it can be found on the internet and in bookshops.

PREPARING YOUR PROPERTY

So far, this book has helped you understand negotiating when you are buying something. This chapter takes the unusual step of helping you get a good deal when you are selling.

Preparation is vital in negotiation – and that includes preparing your property to gain the best price. I will not spend time looking at long-term high investment ideas like loft extensions and new kitchens and bathrooms. Instead, I will suggest quick fixes that should help increase the value of your house or flat.

You need to think about what's in it for the buyers (read Chapter 4 on buying a property to help you see it from their perspective). Often, they enter, thinking: 'Is this a place where I would like to live? Has this got potential? Has it been well kept?' They may even think: 'The décor isn't to my taste, but could we live in this whilst we take our time to change things to our style?' What would you, as a buyer, most value about the place and the people if you were looking for a property?

Here are a few examples of potential cosmetic changes:

1. What about a lick of paint? – Neutral colours will be best as personal taste can differ.

2. Tidy up! – A few hours (or maybe days, depending!) of spring cleaning, tidying up and de-cluttering could have

benefits. Replace any broken bulbs – there's nothing worse than showing someone around at night with a torch! If you haven't the room, speak to a friend who can 'store' some stuff while you show people around, or pay for storage.

3. Freshen up with flowers, and cut the lawn, put in window boxes, tidy garden, etc.

4. Clean the front door and pathway – first impressions count.

5. Put a throw on the sofa – but only if the throw is in better condition than the sofa!

WHAT PRICE TO PUT YOUR PROPERTY ON THE MARKET FOR?

Whether you go through an estate agent or sell privately, putting the property on the market for the right price is important. Sell yourself short – and you can lose thousands of pounds. Aim too high — and you could take ages to sell and still have to come down in price.

Research the websites that specialise in real estate value and look at the local papers' property sections to give you an indication of the price of houses similar to yours in your area.

When you have decided on the price, think of reasons why your house or flat is worth the amount you want to charge. What is it that makes you feel it warrants that price, or makes it especially attractive compared with others in the area? Is it that the road you live in is quieter and more sought after than the neighbouring roads? Have you done any recent renovation work? Preparing these justifications could come in very handy later on in conversations with potential buyers, especially if they are interested in your house, but object to the price.

CHOOSING YOUR ESTATE AGENT

If you decide to use an estate agent, you need to make sure you choose one that suits your needs. It may not necessarily be just about what price they put your house on the market for: i.e. just because they suggest the highest price doesn't mean they're the best. They could be, or maybe they haven't a clue about the area, and are guessing high to get your business.

Estate agents tend to suggest valuations. If you like the agent, but the price they are suggesting does not meet your needs, you can always negotiate. For example:

'If you put the property on the market for £500,000, then we will agree to use you.'

Create your own criteria sheet, listing what is important to you when deciding upon an estate agent.

Take time to get them to come over and value the property, and effectively interview them to ensure they meet the criteria you have set out. If none do, you may have to review your list!

Choosing an estate agent
• understanding of local area
• tailor my own commission rate
• ideal sale at £500,000
• minimum price of £495,000
• allows me to speak to buyers directly (if the buyers are OK with it)
• I feel 'I would buy' from this salesperson

Listing your criteria for choosing an estate agent.

SUGGESTING YOUR OWN COMMISSION STRUCTURE

Once you have agreed what price to put the property on the market for, you can start to consider the agent's fee, as although the percentage may seem small, it soon adds up to significant sums. For example, a sole agent fee of 1.5% on a £500,000 house comes to £7,500. In the UK, you also need to add VAT, which at 17.5%, will increase the amount you pay to £8,812.50. In this case, negotiating even 0.25% will save you £1,250 (£1,468 including VAT). One way of achieving this or of making the system work in your favour is to suggest to the estate agent that you establish your own commission structure or bonus scheme. There is nothing in the rules to stop you doing this. For example:

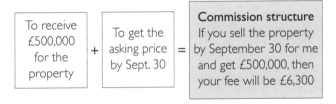

An example of matching your needs to a commission structure that suits you.

If you do set a date for closing the deal, agree what action you will take after that date. Either way, get the re-structured commission structure in writing before you sign up.

Obviously, agents are completely entitled to say no, but if you make the structure sensible and include a genuine incentive for them, you have more likelihood of succeeding. Make sure you cover all eventualities, for example:

Sell the property for	by	Bonus/Commission paid
£500,000	September 30	£6,300 (1.26%)
£498,000	September 30	£5,500 (1.1%)
£497,000	September 30	£5,000 (1%)
£495,000	September 30	£4,000 (0.8%)

SPEAKING TO A DECISION-MAKER

A decision-maker is someone who has the authority to say yes or no to company decisions. It does largely depend on the decisions you want to make as to how high up the ladder you need to go in an estate agent's: in a small outlet, perhaps as far as a partner or owner; in a large multi-shop company, maybe the manager. This is especially relevant when you want to negotiate commission rates, as only they are likely to have the authority to change the terms of the deal.

Finding the best route to speaking to a decision-maker can be tricky: you do not want to upset the individual assigned to you, as their skills may be of use later on in the sale. So always think of it from their perspective: if I were in their shoes, hearing that the customer wants to speak to my boss, how would it be best received?

The example on the next page implies you may move your business elsewhere, if your requests are not met, but it doesn't commit you to it.

You:	Agent thinks:
'Hi Steve. I think you would be great selling my property and I have every confidence in you doing so, but your commission rate is likely to stop me from using you. I realise that Karen Masters heads up the agency and before I potentially move my business elsewhere, I would like to speak to her about this and then you to run with the sale after that.'	Mmmm … he obviously rates me, which is nice to hear. I am not in a position to negotiate commission rates, however Karen will be really pleased I have not lost us business and she has the opportunity of saving it. He values me enough to tell her he wants me to negotiate the business.

HORSES FOR COURSES

When you have chosen your estate agent, allow the specialist salespeople to show the prospective buyers around, if you feel they can do a good job.

Whoever is going to be the primary seller, make sure you get to know them, and as much as possible, gain a good rapport (see Chapter 3), as this could prove invaluable. Also, it is worth asking them to feed back information on the comments of the prospective buyers, which will help the sale go through at the price you want.

THE VIEWING

There are several benefits to being at home when the potential buyers are coming over. This is especially true when they are seeing the property for the second or even third time, as they have become more serious contenders. This also depends on the state of the market at the time, as in periods of high demand, some people are making offers after just one visit, for fear of losing the property.

A word of caution here: gaining a benefit from being around depends upon your people-skills. By this I mean being unobtrusive, relaxed, subtle, and appearing helpful while not overly pushing for a decision. This is tougher than it sounds, as we are talking about a home that you have heavily emotionally and financially invested in here.

Having given the warnings, I would say the benefits outweigh the negatives, as you often get buying signals (see Glossary) and you are also best equipped to answer any questions they may have about the property.

Typical buying signals include:-

A. Asking if fixtures and fittings are included in the price. This is a heavy indication that they are interested. Think of your answer here. It depends what you want to indicate.

   If there is no way you want to include this in the price and are prepared to lose the sale if it comes to it, then just say:

   'No, the price we are offering is based on the property,'
   and ...

1. *'We are intending taking the fixtures and fittings with us for the new property,'*
   or

2. *'We were intending taking them with us as they are worth around x amount, but we are willing to discuss potentially leaving them behind, if we are able to come to an agreed price.'*

   Example 2 does leave you the option of negotiating with them on the items, but make sure *x* is more than you actually want to settle on, as there is every likelihood that they will want to haggle!

If it is possible you would include them in the price, don't give anything away before you get a commitment or indication of sorts from the buyers. Giving away something for nothing is not a wise thing in negotiation. What would you want to get out of the deal? It may just be a commitment from them to buy the property. If so, maybe say something like:

'Well, not officially; however, if you are keen on buying the property, let us know today, and we may be able to come to an amicable agreement.'

STEALTH TACTIC Think beforehand of any positive comments that could increase the 'desire' for your house or flat. For example, the great view, quietness of the area, closeness of the schools and regularity of the trains. You will increase your chances if you casually drop such information into the conversation rather than reel off a list of great sales points. Natural, stealth-like (under the radar) selling will have greater benefits than the go-getting city slicker approach!

B. When they are openly planning what they would do with the rooms.

Who would have which bedroom? What colour curtains? etc. They are effectively measuring up, and, as long as the conversation is flowing between them, i.e. the other person is answering positively, you are well on your way to a sale.

C. If they make themselves comfortable. Maybe they sit down. If they don't, but seem to be asking questions about the house or area that indicate interest, offer them a cup of coffee and make them feel at ease. The more they feel comfortable and at home, the more likely they are to want to make it *their* home!

Having said all that, if you cannot be around, quiz the agent as to what the prospective buyers say during the visit.

BE CAUTIOUS OF WHAT YOU GIVE AWAY

STEALTH TACTIC

Be aware of a selling *faux pas*. If people know that you need to sell quickly, they tend to realise that a bargain may be had. Informing buyers or estate agents of having the need to complete by a certain date or to be at your new location to start your new job in a month can indicate a 'desperate sell'. When you can afford to, be cautious with what you say and use other 'urgent tactics' that may be relevant. This could be merely getting on with it before you change your mind!

If you get to set your own commission rate, a selling deadline may be something that you include automatically (see earlier in this chapter).

CLOSING THE DEAL

Now at this stage, you have either got a keen agent working on your behalf, with whom you have hopefully built up a rapport; or you are negotiating directly with the buyer. Either way, you are in a position to close, and there may be an opportunity to bargain.

Bargaining usually occurs after the buyer raises an objection: in a lot of cases, it is price. In which case, an alternative price could be offered by the buyer, or they could just say that it's too expensive and want you to make another proposal.

I am going to deal with these two scenarios separately; however, versions of these tactics can be applied to each.

A. When they just say the price is too high

Objections like these often mean they are interested and are either using an experienced negotiator's tactic, or offering a signal that they would like to buy, but at a better price. I would normally recommend getting an offer out of them before you continue, but let's assume they won't. What you can then do is ask a question of your own. For example:

'Really, compared with what?'

This will help you get to the crux of the objection.

They may reply:

'Our budget of £495,000.'

So you know their budget, and now you can probe further:

'If price wasn't a problem, would you buy the property?'

'Yes, definitely.'

Now you know that if you overcome this objection, you are likely to be on your way to that semi-detached you set your heart on! You also know that (assuming this is going to be **their** home), they have developed some emotional attachment as well, and unless they physically cannot borrow any more, there is a good chance it's not their final offer.

As price is likely to be the main objection, it is worth having in mind some of your arguments to overcome this, and also the benefits that are linked with them. The problem may need to be probed further, for example:

'I am assuming you have an additional budget for fixtures and fittings?'

If the answer's yes, then you could ask how much they budgeted for kitchen electricals, carpets, curtains, sofas (or indeed anything else you weren't intending to take with you). They may say £5,000 – well, then there may be a compromise to be had with your items:

'If we were to allow you to keep our fixtures and fittings, would you be able to include that in your budget to achieve £500,000?'

If they are willing to go as far as £498,000, then you are only £2,000 away from your ideal return – or even less, if you have restructured the agency commission as explained earlier.

Perhaps they are renting, and think the process could take a few months, and in the meantime have to pay their landlord

£2,000. Saving this could increase their offer to £497,000. Tell them that if they agree now, you can move earlier – and then your ideal return is only £3,000 away.

B. If they offer an alternative price

Brilliant – they're interested!

It is important to find out what is the reason behind the lower offer. Is it because they physically cannot borrow any more? Or do they feel that is what your property is worth?

Listen to the reason and look for a solution.

If they feel the property is simply not worth the value you have placed on it, you can respond (unaggressively, note) with the justifications which you have prepared in advance. For example:

Our property is worth £500,000 because …

1. *'Three-bedroomed properties in the area have consistently been selling for between £490,000 and £500,000 over the past few months. Property inflation has increased by one precent in just the past month, adding a further £5,000.'*
2. *'Ours is in exceptionally good condition (unlike many on the market). It has a recently renovated kitchen and a garden that has been well maintained.'*
3. *'Two streets away the council tax is £500 more a year!'*
4. *'Our neighbours are wonderful; there is no noise at night, even at weekends, as the avenue is well set back from the main road. This is not the case with most of the 'for sale' properties in this area.'*

THE SIXTY-FOUR MILLION DOLLAR QUESTION

When do you close the deal?

There is no one answer to this, as there are many different types of buyers and sellers.

I have always detached myself emotionally from a house when I have been selling, and this allows me to take risks. Obviously, I have wanted to maximise my income, but have always felt sure that if I didn't get an acceptable price, someone else would come along; or, alternatively, I would rather not sell. This is why having a 'walk-away rate' is useful, as when it goes lower, you know what to do, and everything above it is a bonus!

My advice is: if you cannot bear the thought of losing the sale, then make sure you don't. If you feel you are being ripped off, negotiate until you feel comfortable. If you are keen to get a good deal, and are not fussed as to whether you sell now or in six months' time – push it as far as you can go. Interpreting the state of the property market will help clarify things, and a careful eye should be kept on this when making decisions.

WHAT IF I FEEL THE AGENT IS PUSHING ME TO AGREE, WHEN THERE MAY BE MORE TO GET?

Well, hopefully, you have managed to build a rapport with the agent to try to prevent this from happening. However, they are there to sell a property and move on to the next, and you may still find them putting pressure on you.

Perhaps when they say: 'It would be wise to accept £496,000', you could reply:

'I think you have really done a great job so far [making them feel good about what they have done 'so far']. *However, £4,000 is really important to me, as I need this for a down-payment on the house I am buying* [or similar – appealing to emotions]. *I would really appreciate it if you could get this extra money, though of course I don't want to lose the sale – can you give it a try? What do you think are your chances of achieving this?'* [appealing to their sales skills].

WHAT IF THE ESTATE AGENT OR BUYER SAYS: 'THAT IS THE FINAL OFFER – TAKE IT OR LEAVE IT'?

Decision time! In business, I have frequently heard this said when I, as the seller, have turned away custom because the deal was not right for us – only to find the client coming back with a better offer a few days later! However, if you want to sell, and are happy to accept the current offer, then you are at the very least taking risks if you try and push it further. The only possible exception is if you are lucky enough to be speaking to the buyer directly: gauge the reality of this statement there and then; make the difference seem small and that it's a joint problem; and offer the opportunity of a compromise. For example:

You: *'I really want to sell to you, and we are only £2,000 apart – it seems ludicrous, in a £500,000 deal, to fall out over such a relatively small amount, but it's a lot to both of us. If I were to suggest a compromise, would you be in a position to consider it?'*

If you use this or a similar approach, try to do the deal there and then, so as not to let them go away and have second thoughts. You may be OK with it; they could just decide to buy somewhere else!

LOOKING FOR SOLUTIONS TO OTHER PROBLEMS

Moving house is considered one of the biggest stresses in life (along with getting married, changing job and having a baby – I knew someone who did all four at once!) and the more tactics and solutions you can put in place to make the deal seamless, the better.

Look at ways to solve potential problems that may occur. For example, you may be in a position to buy and also have got someone to purchase your house; however, somewhere down the line there is someone holding up the deal. This can result in you losing the property you want.

In this case, consider what you could do. Can you locate the chain-breaker? Then, can you find out what the reason is? Is it that they need to buy carpets and wardrobes, and that comes to £3,000, but they can't get an increase in their mortgage? Can you and the other members of the chain provide a solution? If it is in everyone's interest to provide a solution that will conclude the deal, then what's wrong with that?

IN SUMMARY

1. Prepare your property for sale. A lick of paint here and a tidy-up there will pay dividends.

2. If you decide not to sell privately, choose an estate agent wisely. Go for one that you feel will have your interests at heart, one that you trust. List what is important to you in choosing your agents and stick to it.

3. Think about a commission structure that suits you and suggest this to your prospective agents. You are within your rights to do this.

4. When possible, be present when a buyer is coming round. Your presence and conversation can really influence the likelihood of a sale if used effectively, and also allow you to listen out for buying signals.

5. Objections are good things – it means they are interested. Think of possible objections and your answers, before you negotiate. Listen to their point, probe to get more detail and offer your solutions. In selling, when you have answered all their objections, it often leads to a sale.

6
Booking hotels and holidays

SETTING THE SCENE

A 48-bed hotel in Torquay one chilly afternoon early in October.

'Hello, is that Reservations?'

'Yes sir, how may I help?'

'I would like to book a room for two nights on November 16 and 17. It's two years since my wife and I stayed with you and we got engaged. I suppose you are fully booked, aren't you?'

'Well, actually we have one room left for those nights.'

'Oh fantastic, can you hold on to it for me whilst I check a few more things?'

'Unfortunately not sir, we only have one room left and it's £95 per night per person.'

'Wow that's expensive; I don't suppose you could do it for less, could you?'

'No sir.'

'OK then, I will book it. Is breakfast included?'

'No sir, that will be an additional £10 per person.'

*'Ah, OK, I need breakfast so I will pay for that as well.
I assume it's Full English.'*

'No sir. That will be an additional £5 per person.'

'Ah, OK, I'll have that as well.'

'Can I just confirm you want the booking sir.'

'Yes absolutely.'

'So that's £440+£2 telephone booking fee ...'

'Oh I didn't know that wasn't included.'

'... a total of £442 for two nights ...'

SOUND FAMILIAR?

A break away can be started well before you pack your bags. A holiday is made sweeter if you have booked a great-value deal or indeed had some extras added in to make it even more special.

So what's wrong with the above? Nothing – if you don't mind paying top whack! Below are five areas that led to that expensive deal being struck:

1. You gave specific dates and a **huge** emotional reason as to why you wanted those dates and the real desire to stay at that specific hotel. This will ring pound signs to most salespeople.

2. You told them you thought they were fully booked – this

just restates to them that you would feel honoured if they could get you in.

3. When checking to see if they would bargain, your assumption was that they wouldn't: 'I don't suppose you could do it for anything less, could you?'

4. You confirmed you wanted the room, and indeed agreed the price, **before** you checked or tried to **include** the added extras, i.e. breakfast and telephone charge.

5. What is the likelihood that a 48-bed hotel is fully booked for November (bar one room) five weeks prior to your dates? This is certainly low season in the UK.

THE BENEFITS OF NEGOTIATING

• Better hotels or guesthouses for your budget

• Upgraded rooms at no extra cost

• Dinner included for a B&B price

• Three breaks away for the cost of two

• Free wine with your meal

• A happy partner who loves being taken away!

WHAT'S IN IT FOR THEM

When looking at whether someone is willing to deal lower than an advertised hotel price, you first have to look at 'what's in it for them'. If there is a significant benefit to them, there is more likelihood that they will be willing to trade with you.

Although in their ideal world, hoteliers would gain the quoted rate for your break, what is key to them, especially if they are not over 80% booked, is your custom. Having too many vacant rooms is non-profitable, and the look of lack of occupancy may put off other guests. A fully booked hotel looks popular and makes people feel reassured with their choice.

The hoteliers realise that your pound is key to them, not only now, but also for potential repeat business and referrals. Generally speaking, they would rather have your business than turn it away or, worse still, see you go to a rival hotel.

Many hoteliers will be happy to negotiate, even if it's in a small way, to gain your business. Be polite but confident, and make sure you know what you want before you pick up the phone and ask.

WHAT IS IMPORTANT TO YOU

Knowing what you want to achieve before you book is central to a great-value break. What is important to you? Is it cheap accommodation, quality accommodation at a lower price, or a break that has meals all-inclusive?

List your key objectives and work from there.

Do read both sections here (on cheap and quality accommodation). I have listed some different tactics in each that may still prove useful whichever route you are deciding.

LOOK AT ALL RESOURCES

Research is the key to finding the right accommodation that suits your needs. Use all the resources available to you.

Internet: The internet is a marvellous tool for hunting for bargain accommodation. Use the search engines on the internet (Google, MSN, Ask and Yahoo, etc.) to find the accommodation that suits your needs. With these engines you can be specific about what you want. For example, if you type 'Yorkshire Dales farmhouse self catering', it will automatically list sites that include all or some of these words, helping you to define what you want.

Be aware of sponsored links and advertised sites that often appear at the top or the side, as these people have paid to be on this section and have to account for advertising costs when they offer you prices for accommodation. They may still offer great value, but it's worth noting. I have often found great places on the second and third pages of search engines.

Newspapers and magazines. Scour the travel sections (hidden gems are often found in the classified area).

Specialist books. Local libraries and bookstores are full of B&B, hotel, cottage and guest house directories.

'Phone a friend'. Friends are a good resource for the right accommodation, and you can be assured of an honest critique!

Tourist boards. They will be happy to send you information about local accommodation in their area and will tell you how central the locations are.

Use as many resources as time and inclination will allow. The benefits of this research will be borne out both in the holiday enjoyment and also, hopefully, the price.

Look for special deals, as this gives you further proof that these companies are keen to trade below the full rate dependent upon certain circumstances, e.g. time of year, day of week, etc.

CHEAP ACCOMMODATION

Before you call the hotel, list the questions you want to ask and also have in mind what you want to achieve. For example, have you a specific price in mind? The hotel is advertising a room at £35 per night; you would really love to stay three nights for no more than £75. Think about what you would be happy to settle on – would £90 be acceptable?

When negotiating deals, it is important that you have at least three outcomes in mind. Firstly, your opening offer – one that you would be really pleased with achieving (still within the realms of possibility though!), i.e. in this case £75. Secondly, your good result – one that you are happy with, i.e. £85. Finally, your 'walk-away' rate – where any higher than this will be unacceptable to you: perhaps here, £95.

When you call them, ask for general availability around the date you want rather than saying you want to book a room for a specific date. This will show that you have a vague interest in booking but are not setting your heart on it! The keener you sound, the more they will feel you will book it at the rate offered.

Get their availability and say it's only speculative at the moment, but you will come back to them if you are going to book. Ask them whether, if you felt that the price was a little too high, would it be worth calling if they needed to 'shave' a little off. This will give you a good indication if they are willing to trade.

This has several good negotiation effects:

1. Saying it's only speculative implies that you are going to

consider your options rather than definitely give them the booking.

2. Saying that you will come back to them if you are going to book is key to what you are **not** saying. A good salesperson will pick up what you have **not** said. You can't rely upon this, but there is a good chance it will have the desired effect.

You:	Seller thinks:
'I will come back to you if I am going to book.'	Mmm … so what he's implying is that if he isn't happy with the deal he will not call us back. I don't want to lose this deal.

Implied statements can be effective.

When you have done your homework and got several options, look at the best prices and call back the top two or three (especially if they said they were willing to trade).

You can then say you are aware that the rate is usually £105 and you did promise to get back if you were still interested. You are still keen, but the rate is too high; however, you would be willing to look at £75 for three nights (don't say 'book' unless you intend to, as this really is making what is known as a 'conditional offer' – see Glossary at the back of the book). They may agree, or offer you a counter proposal.

When you are sure of the hotel you wish to stay at, you can then make them a firm offer. Say that if they are willing to offer the room at £x, you are then in a position to book straight away.

STEALTH TACTIC It can be useful to have a few questions or statements to hand that you think you already know the answer to. This could help you gain a better deal. For example, 'Breakfast is included isn't it?' You think at that price it may not be; however, a) you could be pleasantly surprised, or b) it isn't, but as you have mentioned it as something you thought **was** included, they could feel on the back foot, as a salesperson does not like to answer 'no' when they are trying to convert a sale.

QUALITY ACCOMMODATION

What does quality mean to you?

Is it the rooms or the facilities?

Is it the Michelin-star restaurant?

Is it the location?

Once you know this, you know what's important to you in the negotiation and you evaluate with this in mind.

As with 'cheap accommodation', it is important to do your homework beforehand, but this time with your 'quality' look on things. Search the internet, ask the hotels to send you brochures so you can get a feel of the place, ask friends if they have stayed there before – what had they noticed? Ask the hotel also to send details of any specials they have on offer, e.g. Valentine's weekend. Although you may not be booking that particular weekend, you will still get a feel of what additional items they offer so that you could try and get them to include these in the price. This could be flowers and Champagne in the room or a massage and a manicure.

Also ask the hotel to send details of any specials in terms of price – this will give you an idea of how low they will publicly go! For example, they may have a current offer of three nights for £200 when their normal rate is £100 per night. From this you know that they are willing to sell rooms at just over £65 per night under certain conditions.

Once you have done your preparation, call the hotel again about general availability over a few weeks and the prices. Be aware that a good salesperson may tell you there is 'limited availability' in order to get you to commit.

STEALTH TACTIC It may be worth ringing up and asking for five rooms on a particular weekend, e.g. for a wedding anniversary celebration. If the clerk seems to see this as no problem, then you have your answer as to whether the availability really is limited.

Once you have got all the information you need and you have prioritised your hotels in order of preference, ring your top three choices starting with your third. Let them know the date(s) you are thinking about and ask for the price. You will already know about their availability, and remember – a hotel does not like empty rooms!

Let them know you have researched other hotels in the area and you are **considering** booking theirs. At this point you should raise an objection and offer them a potential solution, e.g. price.

'Compared with some of my choices, you are £20 per night more expensive. If I were to stay three nights instead of 2, would you give me a £60 discount?'

You may fully intend to stay three nights, but that doesn't matter – you are offering them a deal.

By using this approach, you are not committing to the deal; you are only offering up an idea. At this point, they can say no, yes or offer an alternative.

If the answer is no, ask them if there is anything else that they can offer. If yes, say that it sounds good and you need to discuss things and will be back to them by a specific date, if you are booking (this may spark them to considering bettering the deal again if you book now – then the choice is yours!). If they offer something else, then you can consider it and get back to them later.

If successful with your third choice, you can then do the same with your second choice and perhaps chance your arm a little further, finally leaving yourself a great deal as an alternative (BATNA – see Glossary for more details) if your number one choice doesn't wish to trade.

Now you have choices when you go to your ideal hotel. You are free to tell them what great deals you have been offered elsewhere. Say you would love to stay at their hotel but the price is too high – will they price match/beat? If they won't price match, will they be able to offer something that suits your requirements? Will they come down on their price and 'throw in' some goodies? What can they do to get your custom?

When you are at the end of the negotiation (but not before), remember to tell them if it's a special anniversary or event, as they may add in some extra touches, and often they are happy to 'throw them in' as a deal closer if asked. For example, if it's your wedding anniversary and you tell them, you may find that

Choice 3	Choice 2	Choice 1
You: 'Your rates are £20 per night more than my budget will allow. If I were to stay three nights instead of two, would you offer me a £60 discount?' Hotelier : 'Yes, but we would need to know soon.' You: 'I will let you know in the next two hours if I intend to book. Thank you for your help.'	You: 'I like your hotel and what it has to offer, but the Conrad will offer £120 a night. I realise your hotel is superior, but you're £50 a night more expensive. If I stayed three nights instead of two, could you offer me £120?' Hotelier: 'We couldn't price match but would be happy to offer a rate of £130 a night instead of £170 and include breakfast.' You: 'OK thank you, it's slightly more than I am happy to pay but I will consider your offer. Can I let you know within the next hour if I am to go ahead?'	You: 'You are my number one choice of hotel, but I cannot ignore the exceptional deals that your rival hotels have offered; however, I did say I would call back if interested, but I need some help with the price.' Hotelier: 'Thank you madam. How can we help?' You: 'If you can offer me a deal of £120 inclusive of breakfast, then I can book three nights instead of two.' Hotelier : 'Our rate is £200 per night inclusive of breakfast, but in the light of what you are saying, I will offer £130 per night all-inclusive.' You: 'Well you are my first choice, I am happy to book at that and thank you.'

Example conversations with hotels.

you get an upgraded room or a chilled bottle of Champagne left in your room to help you celebrate.

Rest assured, if you approach hoteliers in the right way, they will be only too happy to accommodate you (excuse the pun!). Remain positive, polite and seemingly flexible and they will welcome you with open arms!

OTHER WAYS OF GETTING THE PRICE DOWN

If you can possibly offer two or three alternative dates to them in return for a better price, this will also help, as it means they can check their room vacancies and match them with the dates you offer.

Prices will vary depending on the season; however, even in peak season deals can be made, especially at the last minute. Most people book summer holidays in advance, but if hotels and guest houses have availability at short notice, they are much more likely to negotiate. The beauty for you is that if it's in the UK, at least this way you will have a good idea what the weather is going to be like!

Do remember that the best deals are made when both parties are happy, so ensure that you don't push price too far, as a good holiday can also be helped by a co-operative guest house owner.

START LOW AND WORK YOUR WAY UP

In business negotiation, experts often discuss trading on something small at first, and then dangle the carrot of additional business to the seller to gain a better overall price.

Within accommodation, this can be used to great effect. Why

not negotiate for a two-night stay, and when you are happy with the price see what you can get for a third night?

ADDITIONAL EXTRAS

Maybe this is more important to you than price, in which case the tactics above can work exactly the same way. Maybe you want dinner included or Champagne in the room on arrival, instead of money off or a half-day excursion. Hotels offer many additional services (see figure below). The same principle applies: you just need to know what you want out of the deal before you try and get it.

Always tell people what you want: it puts you in the driving seat. But to make sure you are in pole position, start by asking for even more!

In-room additions	Hotel amenities	External deals

• Champagne
• wine
• chocolates
• flowers
• internet
• films
	• free gym
	• treatments
	• meals
	• laundry
	• newspaper
		• excursions
		• bike hire
		• transfers to
		  destination
		  e.g. airport

Examples of additional extras supplied by hotels.

PACKAGE DEALS

I have focused more on individual breaks away rather than package deals as there is often more scope here. DIY holidays (where you book each part separately – now referred to as 'dynamic packaging') tend to be easier to negotiate and offer more flexibility.

However, package deals have potential for negotiation as well. Some travel agents will be more willing than others, but similar principles apply. Good preparation and an understanding of various companies' offerings will help you whittle down the list, as similar holidays can often be had with different tour operators, and prices vary.

If you think that the average holiday abroad will cost around £750 – £1,000 per person, and profit margins tend to be around 10%, there is an amount there that is potentially negotiable. However, once individual shops' operating costs and personal bonus schemes are taken into consideration, this room for manoeuvre comes down.

Prices also vary due to demand, which can be swayed by specific circumstances. For example, great weather conditions at home can mean that prices for package holidays abroad tumble, as people decide to stay in their own country.

It may be possible to negotiate additional extras. Meals on flights are not always included now, and insurance often has high mark-ups (though looking at annual insurance can be cost efficient, if you travel more than once in a year).

BLOCK BOOKING HOTELS

Sometimes, perhaps for a wedding or a party, you want to offer guests/friends a choice of three or four hotels/guesthouses to stay at. If you are recommending people stay in certain locations, then you can supply a 'fact sheet' of local information. With this, you are effectively offering the accommodation choices free advertising. In return for this, why not ask for a discount, or perhaps even a free room for you to use, either then or at a later date?

Let's take a wedding as an example. Research the locations you would like potentially to use, and a couple of good alternatives just in case the main choices don't want to negotiate. Do some research on each of your choices, listing their benefits, pricing, etc. (see earlier on in this chapter for more detail). Be aware that if you choose peak season and/or a weekend, then the room for negotiation is likely to be less than if it is either off-peak or mid-week.

Think of what it is you want in return for listing their hotel as one of your preferred accommodation points. For example, can they discount the rate? Have later check-out times? Offer you a free room if 15 or more people stay at the location (either for the wedding or as a treat to you and your partner a few months later)?

Have in your mind at least two outcomes: firstly, your ideal one – what it would be great to get; and secondly, your 'walk-away' outcome – going below that price would make you use an alternative.

Ideal	Walk-away
• price £50 per person	• price £85 per person
• check-out 12 pm	• check-out 11 am
• free room for a night for us (including breakfast) if eight or more rooms booked	• if 15 rooms or more booked, a free night for us (including bed and breakfast)
• breakfast 7–10 am	

Two outcomes of a block-booking deal.

With this detail, write up what you intend to put on your fact sheet about them **if** they agree to your terms.

A negotiated point (normally 7.30–9 am). People like flexibility with their breakfast. Some need to leave early, whilst others like a lie-in after a late night! If 20 people are staying (over and above their other quota of guests), then the cook may be able to stagger it over three hours instead of 1.5.

A negotiated point (normally 10 am). People like late check-outs so they do not have to rush in the mornings. This is a big selling point to our guests as they like to get up on a Sunday and take their time. This will probably appeal to at least half of them.

A negotiated point. Ten rooms with 20 people and the hotelier will gain £1,000 per night. Included is a good testimonial from you as well!

A negotiated point – allows hotel to keep track of specific bookings and avoid cheap offers to people who are not wedding guests.

Hotel de Lux

4-star boutique hotel. All en-suite rooms, tea and coffee in room, full English breakfast served at your leisure between 7 and 10 am. Late check-out time of 12 pm for Smith guests. Rooms normally £100 per person per night: specially negotiated rate of £50 per person per night.
'A quality hotel at a fantastic rate!'
Telephone 01234 567890 and quote Smith Special.

An example of an advertisement on the fact sheet and the benefits to both parties.

Do this for all your intended accommodation points. I would suggest limiting the number that you put on the list, as this is the unique point for the location, and the less competition they have for your friends' and family's business, the more enticing it will be for them. So, if there are 20 hotels in the area, limit the number you list to around five, so that the hotels have a real incentive to be included. You may want to pick five that offer different pricing and facilities, ranging from the luxurious, with pool and gym and large en-suite bedrooms, down to a local bed and breakfast, more suitable for the smaller budget.

Then call (or meet face-to-face) your ideal locations and let the negotiations begin! Make sure you are speaking to a decision-maker when you are negotiating, as, if you speak to a junior member of staff, it's likely they won't have the authority to adjust the details of a deal. An example conversation for the above could go (assuming all the pleasantries of introductions have occurred):

'We are currently preparing for our wedding on August 31, and are putting together a fact sheet that will go out to 120 guests, most of whom will need accommodation for either one or two nights. Although there are over 20 locations for us to choose from, we are only telling them of five. Our choice of locations will be made by the ones that will offer what we feel are reasonable packages and listen to our needs. The five will spread across a range of prices and quality. As one of four hotels in the area that we deem as 'high-quality', yours is very much one of them. If we were to advertise you in our fact sheet, would you be willing to offer us a special deal?'	This gives them the detail, setting out the number of guests who could be interested in their hotel, and that you have a range to choose from. Also, you are happy to consider them as the only 4-star hotel (flattering them in the process) advertised, **if** they are interested in doing a deal. You can chop and change the wording to suit the location **but** remember to make it sound interesting. Tempt them in such a way that they want to hear more.

Let's assume they are interested. They could, at this stage, make you an offer. If so, consider it against your ideal outcome; it may even be better! If they ask you what you would like, then phrase it similarly to below:

'Well, I have taken the trouble to write some wording for the advert; it contains what I believe will entice our friends to stay with you. If you are happy with the information within it, then all we would want in return for that is a guarantee, that when eight rooms are taken, you give us a free night's stay with breakfast, and, if more than 15 rooms are taken, the offer is extended to two nights.'	This is likely to create interest with them as they will probably (unless fully booked) want to hear more on how you can deliver them occupancy of 15 or more rooms at little or no cost. The deal also has an incentive in it for you to 'sell' as many rooms on their behalf as you can, with the bonus of a two-day stay for you.

If the answer is yes, then read out the copy. If no, ask them what they would consider.

If they do not wish to consider a deal, politely thank them for their time, then go to one of your alternative quality hotels and go through a similar process, hopefully getting the deal that suits you and your guests.

Remember that if they say no to your proposal and offer an alternative, you can always say that you will consider their offer and let them know in the next few days. It may be worth asking whether, if you needed them to slightly better the deal, they would want you to call them back before making a decision. If they say yes, then it's likely you can get a little bit extra from them. If no, you know you have pushed them to their limits.

The idea of designing an advertisement is merely an example and may not be for you. The most successful negotiators are ones who use their personality and style to persuade others. You may just wish to tell them what you want and go from there.

IN SUMMARY

1. Research the accommodation in the area where you want to stay. Decide upon what's important for you to have. Also have a list of additional extras, including added touches to the room, for example: chocolates and Champagne. Is the accommodation you are looking for cheap and cheerful, or is it luxury hotels? Be clear about what you want to achieve.

2. Refine your list to perhaps three locations. List their strengths and weaknesses, as well as what you would like to pay for each and have included in the price. Look at any special offers that they have recently had to help indicate their likelihood to negotiate.

3. When speaking to each location, use the information that you have researched to persuade them to offer you a good rate, or alternatively, make a proposal yourself (again, be clear in your mind what you want to achieve). Preparing in advance what you are going to say to them can be very useful.

4. Use your list of additional extras to add those final extra touches to the deal BEFORE you agree to the booking.

7

The wedding negotiator

Having been involved in delivering marriage lessons for pre-wedding couples, I understand that there is much to discuss before the big day. Within the sessions, we have often discussed the 'three Rs': Relationships, Religion and Reproduction. You'll be grateful to hear that none of the 'three Rs' is up for discussion within this book!

However, there is also a 'fourth R' that should be mentioned at the very outset, and that's the 'Ridiculous cost' that weddings can involve. As the day takes months and often years of planning, why not spend a bit of extra time, and give yourself the opportunity of saving hundreds and maybe even thousands of pounds?

BENEFITS OF NEGOTIATING

1. Cut down wedding costs – saving for example 10% on a £20,000 wedding.

2. Free additional items that will increase the quality of the function: for example, a calligrapher or personalised matchbooks.

3. Additional add-ins to be enjoyed after the event. For

example, a free weekend at the hotel the wedding reception is being held at, including dinner, bed and breakfast – maybe on your first anniversary.

Below are a few examples of cost areas for a wedding and, as you can see, if we were to dedicate time and space to all of them, the book could just be about weddings (but if you feel there's the need, write to me care of the publishers, and I will get busy typing!).

Pre-wedding	Wedding	Post-wedding
outfits (bride/groom)	flowers	site fees for reception
outfits (bridesmaids/best man, ushers)	music	food
invitations and response cards	cars to/from wedding	drink/corkage
hairdressers	transport to/from reception	flowers
outfits (page boys etc.)	photographer	wedding cake
bouquets	video	music

Virtually all the products or services at a wedding have potential for negotiation.

Also, the more that you can buy in one place – for example, outfits – the more likelihood there is to be an opportunity for negotiating, because suppliers will be more willing to bargain if they see a big order potentially coming their way.

To save time and paper, we will highlight some key areas and expand upon them; this should give you an idea of how to negotiate all aspects of the wedding.

The two we will focus on are: stationery, and the wedding reception (assuming food and drink are from the same supplier). I have covered block booking of hotels in Chapter 6. Be aware that the prices are fictional and should not be used as a benchmark for budgets.

I. STATIONERY

What do you need?

There is a wide variety of stationery used for a wedding. First, list the items you definitely need to purchase: some that would be nice to have made; and others that either you or a friend could make yourselves (perhaps with a computer and printer). Think of the quantity of each item that you require.

Need-to-buy	Nice-to-have	Make myself
• invitations (whole day) 120	• seating cards 120	• maps 100
• invitations (evening) 60	• thank you paper/ envelopes 100	• local info 90
• responses 180	• matchbooks 80	
• order of service 100	• calligrapher	
• menu cards 120		

An example of a wish-list for stationery, separating must-buy from the rest.

Where can you get them?

Stationers can be located on many high streets, on-line and from the yellow pages or specialist magazines/books. Make sure you think of this very early in the process, as invitations need to be sent out and sometimes the lead-time needed for stationery is longer than you think, and may be even longer depending on the type of printing that you choose.

Which stationers do you choose?

What is important to you?

The paper the items are printed on?

The typeface or type of printing (for example, engraving, thermography or off-set)?

The variety of products that are on offer? From invitations to matchbooks.

Or the price?

If you can choose one supplier, and negotiate a deal with them, it is more likely that you will gain a better discount, as bulk buying invariably improves the price.

Whittle down your list of potential suppliers to perhaps three that offer the products you want, and then create a list like the one opposite.

Planning your strategy

Let's assume that Stationer 1 is your ideal choice, in this case because of the quality and look of the paper. What you want to

Stationer 1	• Does invitation, responses, evening invitations, order of service and menu cards (must-haves). Paper slightly more to my liking than the other two. • Can also do seating cards, matchbooks and supply a calligrapher (all nice-to-haves). Seating cards £20, matchbooks £80, calligrapher £80. • Can deliver in a month, does many other stationery items. Price for must-haves works out at £1,000. Can see samples in shop. • Has the best quality of paper on offer.
Stationer 2	• Does all must-haves and nice-to-haves (can get a calligrapher but will cost £90 more). • Three-week delivery (nice but not a must-have). Will send samples free in post. Overall price for must-haves £1,050. Seating cards £18, matchbooks £75, calligrapher £60.
Stationer 3	• Does all must-haves and nice-to-haves. • 3-week delivery. Will send samples through post. Overall price for must-haves £1,100, will include calligrapher free-of-charge. Seating cards £18, matchbooks £90.

A list of stationers and pertinent information that will help you decide which to choose.

do now is look at valid reasons for the retailers to negotiate with you.

Let's look at the differences between 3 and 1. Stationer 1 doesn't send samples to you; you have to pick them up at the shop (but it is only 15 minutes away from you in a car, so no significant hassle). They charge for a calligrapher, whereas you can get one free with your package with Stationer 3 (although their package price is more expensive). The fact that Stationer 1 takes a month instead of three weeks is neither here nor there as it doesn't matter to you (of course, you have allowed plenty of time!); however, you are looking at reasons for the retailer **to** negotiate, so, being conservative in what you say could have benefits here. Overall, Stationer 1 offers you the best price, but as there are differences throughout, you can use the above information to your advantage, whilst still being truthful.

Start with Stationer 3. Although your third choice, it is often worth establishing the best package you can get for your second and third choice before tackling your first, as it could put you in the best bargaining position, with two great offers to fall back on if necessary.

Prepare your opening statement

Look at all the information you have gathered, put into a statement your 'sales argument' and use it in your conversation with the stationers.

A typical conversation could go ...

You on the phone to Stationer 3:

> *'Hello Jessica, thank you for your prompt quote the other day. Whilst your package is good, it is coming in a bit more expensive for what we need than my other two choices. Also the paper quality is not exactly what I wanted. If it eventually just came down to price, then would you consider £1,100, including the matchbooks and seating cards?'*

Assuming you managed to negotiate a better deal, a similar conversation could be had with Stationer 2.

In both conversations, just ask them if a deal is feasible, but do not offer them the business at this stage, if they agree.

Finally, your conversation with Stationer 1 could be something like:

> 'Hello Steve. I appreciate your quote and the level of service you can offer, though your competitors did offer good service, including sending their samples through the post to me. I would like to use your stationery; however, I have been quoted £1,050 [assuming you managed to discount Stationer 2 to this price] and this includes the calligrapher, matchbooks and seating cards. Price is a real issue to me. I can overcome the longer lead time compared with the other two if I order now. If you did the same package, including calligrapher, matchbooks and seating cards for £1,000, then I would place the business with you now.'

The 'if and then' statement commits you **only** if they agree to your conditions. Equally, it allows you to make further suggestions/offers without looking stupid.

With three choices and three prepared negotiations, you have significantly increased your chances of creating a great deal that is right for you.

2. THE RECEPTION

What to prepare before you negotiate

Although the ceremony itself is of great importance, so, to many people, is the reception. Choosing the right location, menu, wine, table settings and size of room is important, so the list of must-haves and nice-to-haves is very relevant.

Buying a wedding planning book will give you some good hints and tips on what you need to be thinking about. This book is about the negotiation and therefore doesn't claim to be a wedding planning expert!

The prices of receptions can vary; however, if you think that it is quite common to spend £12,000, then it highlights the importance of negotiation, as if you can save even 5%, that amounts to £600.

The list opposite will help you clarify what's important and also what would be nice to have. Equally, be clear in your mind what your budget is whilst putting the list together, as there is no point thinking of gold napkin rings engraved with your names when you are working on a shoe-string budget! Your choice of date can also help: venues tend to be less flexible on pricing at weekends since these are more popular (this can also apply to many other items used for weddings, including photographers and limousine hire).

Choosing your shortlist of venues

Use the list you made (see opposite) to help you short-list your venues. Research your options via the internet, recommendations from friends, your own personal experiences of weddings/parties/ conferences you have been to, yellow pages, newspapers, wedding magazines – the list is endless. Where possible, get the location to send you a brochure with details as well as arranging to go and see them. Although a list is good for criteria-setting, nothing beats having a feel of what the place is like.

Must-have	Nice-to-have
• date either Thursday 10 June or Friday 11 June	• ideally 10 June
• budget under £12,000 to include all must-haves and drink	• all-inclusive price of food, drink (exc. Champagne), room-rental of £11,250
• must accommodate 120 for sit-down and 60 more in evening	• allow external decorators in (flowers, table ornaments)
• no more than five miles from wedding ceremony	• rooms for people to stay
• country setting	• us staying the night there
• allow own Champagne to be bought in (costs to include corkage)	• toastmaster
• extension until 12 am	• extension to 2 am
• reserved parking area for a minimum of 40 cars	• parking for up to 60 cars
• allow an external disco	• complimentary meal for six after the event (as a 'thank you' to parents)
• a dance area	
• waitress service	
• hot main course with vegetarian option	

An example list of must-haves and nice-to-haves at a wedding reception.

Visiting the short-listed venues

Try and visit the venues and the specific rooms on the day of a wedding, and persuade the managers to let you see things both before the event, and with the reception in full flow. This will give you a good feel about how the place copes with a function similar to the one you are holding. You are likely to be spending a significant amount of money on the reception, and therefore you need to be assured that you are picking the right venue.

Questions to ask the short-listed few

Prepare some questions beforehand that will help you decide between your choices. Think of what's important to you to make the event a smooth, happy, successful and memorable one. Here is an example of a set of questions:

'Are both dates available? If so, have you a preference of dates?'	It shows them that you are willing to be flexible, and also fit in with their plans (at this stage you are not giving your reasons for this, but all will become clear when you want to negotiate, as you can use your willingness to fit in with their plans to create a better deal for you).
'I am thinking of maybe bringing in my own choice of wine and Champagne; is this feasible?'	I know! We only initially said our own Champagne. Plans haven't changed, but this is a way of 'managing their expectations', as you can eventually say, 'What if I bought your wine and only used our own selection of Champagnes?' It may allow you to have that extra bartering power. Also note, we didn't mention a corkage fee. Let them talk about this, as no-one likes to talk about additional prices that deliver nothing! You never know, you may get it for free!
'We would like the reception to continue until 2 am; I assume it is OK to keep the bars open until then.'	This is a statement really, however one that says what you would like. People who are selling you their services do not like to say no to things as this has a negative impact, and although this may or may not get you what you want, it certainly increases your chance of negotiation. Listen out for what they **don't** say. For example: '2 am is too late' or 'we would rather not stay open until 2 am.' These statements are revealing a potential

compromise or even agreement. Finding out what is getting in the way of them agreeing to an extension and overcoming their objection may help here. For example, they may say that experience has shown that whenever the bar has been kept open until 2 am, people haven't left the area until 2.30 am. In which case you could say that you are happy for the bar to shut at 1.30 am, and you will personally announce to people that the area is to be vacated by 1.50 am.

'Will we be the only ones using the room that day? Can we get in at 9 am to add the final touches?'	Establishing something like this prior to agreeing to use the venue is vital. This is when you have most negotiating power, as you have not committed, and they are likely to be keen to win your custom. Think of all other similar additions that will be important and useful to you, as this is the time to get the final few extras.
'We like your venue. The décor and atmosphere seem to fit in well with what we want. In fairness, our other two choices seem to offer similar facilities and additional touches that we require. It's a tough choice we have to make here and your corkage fee and one am curfew, along with the fact that you are around £1,000 more expensive, are leaning us towards the others. Is there some movement on these areas that will help us to favour your venue? We will be in a position to book in the next fortnight and will promise to speak to you prior to booking anything else, if you can help out.'	This is only an example, remember, but it gives you an idea of how to formulate a sensible and logical argument to open up a negotiation. You praise their venue, you make them feel they are a real choice; however, you have some genuine reservations that **may** make you choose a competitor over them. Alongside this, you are giving them the opportunity to at least signal their willingness to negotiate, and in return you will agree to speak to them prior to you booking anything else. Nothing ventured – nothing gained!

STEALTH TACTIC

When viewing your short-list of venues, try not to give too many 'buying signals' (see Glossary). It is far too easy to sit there and discuss with whoever you have come with how you could see the venue being your 'ideal location' and let the emotions run riot about 'how great the day will be if you came here.' However, this does tend to take away any negotiation prospects you may have had, as the venue representatives will realise that you are likely to book anyway, regardless of them offering any discounts. Remain keen but open-minded, positive but not committed. Nothing wrong with a bit of good cop/bad cop here: letting your partner play the positive side, whilst you put a slight dampener on things – just make sure you plan it beforehand.

Highlighting the pros and cons of the venue

List the pros and cons of each venue to allow you to prioritise them in terms of choice.

Favourite venue	Venue 2	Venue 3
Can do either date	June 10 only	Can do either date
Can do all musts	Can do all musts	Can do all musts
£10 corkage per bottle (50 bottles +£500)	£8 corkage per bottle (50)	Free corkage up to 30 bottles providing we buy their wine
1 am extension (owners' choice and not legal requirement)	2 am extension	2 am extension
Bedrooms available	Bedrooms available	No bedrooms to book

Toastmaster available for £100	No toastmaster	Will include toastmaster
Total price £12,000 (not inc. Toastmaster) – £12,100	Total price £11,500 (including corkage)	Total price £11,100

Using the pros and cons to negotiate the deal

The table above shows your favourite venue as over-budget and therefore not hitting one of your must-have points; however, it is still your number one, and, with this in mind, we will have to focus on achieving this location within budget. In this instance, venue 3 is well under budget and shows what can be achieved within your lists of must-haves (despite its quality feel not being as good as your favoured venue), and in this case, it can be used as an ideal price to reach.

In this instance, perhaps start with venue 2 and have a conversation like:

'Hi. Thank you for your time the other day and showing us around. We are seriously considering your venue. However, there are a few things we would need to address, if we were to still keep you in mind, and I thought it only fair to discuss this with you. I realise June 11 isn't available; however, this would have been a better choice for us, as it's closer to the weekend. Equally, you can't provide a toastmaster, whereas our other venues can, and one is free of charge, giving us extra value. However, we can accept this and keep you in our considerations, if you can help us on two points. Firstly, corkage of the Champagne is £8, whereas we

*can get it for free elsewhere. For 50 bottles, that adds up
to £400. Also your price is slightly too high anyway.
Whilst we cannot promise to book, if you were to lower
the price by £600 including waiving the corkage, then
we would re-consider and definitely let you know either
way by next Wednesday.'*

In the above conversation, you were completely truthful
(there's no point in highlighting the negative elements to other
deals, we are not in arbitration here!). Equally, you are not
saying you *will* book it at this price, but will merely get back
to them to let them know either way. I am assuming, of course,
that you will do this: good negotiators are honourable
negotiators.

If they say: 'no, it's too much discount', what are they **not**
saying? They are not saying no, **full stop**. They themselves are
indicating that there is a certain amount of discount, but not
£600. In which case, it's fair enough to ask 'what would you
be willing to discount, then?'

Let's assume you manage to negotiate some concessions, say
£400 off. In which case you have what's known as a good
BATNA. A BATNA is a Best Alternative To a Negotiated
Agreement. So if your number one choice does not meet your
requirements, then you can go to venue number 2.

Now you have a price target of £11,100. It is the time to weigh
up what you are prepared to accept from your ideal choice. Is
it £11,100, or will you be willing to pay a little more for it?
Know your route before you go into battle!

Negotiating with your number one choice

Again, have your prepared list in front of you (three venues) with updates based on earlier conversation with venue 2. Prepare your opening statement; an example could be:

'Hi. It was really nice to be shown around the reception room last week. It certainly is up there in our top two choices, and, if we could iron out a few points, then I feel hopeful we could come to an agreement.

Although there are a few other minor points, there are three main areas of concern.

Firstly the corkage. I can get this for free everywhere else and it's only really for a toast and maybe a glass or two before the meal[1], so there will be plenty of drinking over and above that. Could you agree to waiving the fee for this? Secondly, the overall fee is £1,000 more than our other choice, and this seems a lot, and in fact, takes us way over budget[2]. Finally, the one-o'clock extension. You are the only one who is not allowing us to carry on going until 2 am. If you let us go on until 2 am, it means a bigger bar take for you and likely more full breakfasts eaten in the morning![3] If you agree to an extension to 2 am and bring down the overall price (including no corkage fee) to £11,000, then we will book with you now.'

[1] This puts it into perspective, and makes it look a smaller point to them as it seems a small concession when you break it down to the odd glass or two.

[2] Do not reveal your budget, as this, funnily enough, seems to be often the figure that people say they can't go below when they hear it!

[3] Pointing out 'what's in it for them' is so often used effectively in sales.

Try to agree each point in isolation and seek agreement one by one. If not possible, then put them all on the table.

The added extras

Are there other things you would like included? For example, a weekend's stay on the first year anniversary, or a meal for you and the parents after your return from honeymoon. When I got married, we had a meal for ten family and friends in the restaurant a month after the wedding, with all the drink completely free of charge.

Equally, if in the above example you had managed to seek agreement from your favourite venue on each point without offering them the business, then you could use your 'if and then' on the final added extra you wanted. For example: 'If you provide us with an all-inclusive meal for six a month after the wedding, then we will book the venue at £11,000.'

IN SUMMARY

1. List the points at which you need to pay for the products or services.

2. Make sure you give each area a budget you need to achieve.

3. Take a specific area you wish to negotiate – for example, the wedding reception – and separate your must-haves from nice-to-haves.

4. Short-list three or four locations/retailers that fulfil your criteria (from point 3), along with the various prices.

5. Use the list of pricings and offerings to create your sales arguments for a reduction in price or for getting additional items for nothing.

6. Start with your least favourite choice and negotiate with them. Create a good alternative package to your main choice.

7. Negotiate with your main choice, safe in the knowledge that you have a good alternative if you didn't manage to strike the deal you want.

8
Buying a brand new car

Buying a car is an expensive necessity for most people and is very much an area where negotiation skills can help to lower the price. Car salespeople are highly skilled at their job and know more tricks within selling than a lot of other business people. Whether you are buying a new or used vehicle, being able to negotiate can save you thousands of pounds.

My own experience tells me this, having seen another customer pay the full asking price (£15,100) for the same model for which I paid £12,600. He did get some mats thrown in for the price. Mind you, they proved to be very expensive car mats at £2,500 for a set!

SETTING THE SCENE

One chilly Saturday in January, you park your old banger in a car park and stride across to the local showroom, where a salesperson catches your eye and welcomes you to the start of your car purchasing journey.

'Has sir got a model in mind?'

'Yes, I love the new sporty Santina. *Wow, what a model! Fell in love with it straight away.'*

'It is rather nice, isn't it, sir? Did you notice the built-in GPS system?'

'Notice it? It practically leapt out at me and said I know where you want to go, you just sit back and I'll do the rest! I also liked the idea of the CD player, but does it hold more than 6 CDs at a time?'

*'Alas no sir, however the upgraded XTX model handles 12 CDs and uses the latest sub-woofer speakers as well – definitely a must for the successful executive. Along with the metallic blue finish, you will be the envy of the street **and** the boardroom.'*

'Can we go for a test-drive?'

'Of course we can, sir.'

The salesman grabs the keys and off you go, with you in the driver's seat.

'How's it handling?'

'Like a dream, I am practically floating. The temperature is really cool as well.'

'That's the beauty of air conditioning. However, climate control is the way forward for the man who wants the ultimate in car comfort. If you're doing a lot of driving, you need to feel comfortable. Do you like the idea of your perfect climate at the touch of a button?'

'Oh yes!'

'Not a problem, sir. For just an additional £275, you can feel the heat of Hawaii in the winter, or the freshness of Finland in the summer.'

'I want it, but it seems expensive.'

'Well, John, may I call you John? [a nod from you]. If you buy the car today, and today only, you can take advantage of our fantastic low interest loan. That way I can lose the £275, and the car will be totally yours in three years' time.'

'Really, so I'll get it for free. Fantastic, let's go do the paperwork!'

ASSESSING THE ABOVE

1. Don't get too excited. For some people, it's hard not to when purchasing a new car. Advertising is designed to arouse people's emotions about a vehicle and its extras, and the industry spends millions of pounds on it each year. They do this because the market is very competitive, and they want to get you into their showroom focused on their brand and a particular model.

   They know their target audience (the people who normally buy their cars) including typical age-group, and have a reasonable idea what your lifestyle is like as they have done research on this.

   Too much excitability can give the salesman vital clues about your intention to buy. However, if you go to the other extreme (i.e. suggest that you couldn't care less) then this will also arouse suspicion as it's rare to spend anything upwards of £7,000 without some sort of emotion.

2. Be aware of ego-boosting comments. A good salesperson wants to gain rapport with his or her customer (see Chapter 3). A compliment or a sense of understanding your needs is a great technique used to get you relaxed and in buying

mode. This, however, can also be used to your advantage, as we will see later on in the chapter.

3. Don't list all your wants straight away. If you tell a salesperson about all the bells and whistles that you want included, they will naturally add them on at full price. Leaving this element until later in the deal will give you much more bargaining power.

4. Define low-interest! If you are offered special interest deals, go through them in fine detail to make sure you are better off and not paying more than you need to. Many car companies offer 0% interest deals at various points during the year.

THE BENEFITS OF NEGOTIATING

1. Gaining a better price for your car and possibly saving yourself thousands of pounds.

2. An upgraded model for the price of the basic one.

3. Added extras either included in the price or heavily discounted.

4. A free tank of fuel.

5. Potentially better trade-in rates for your old car.

WHAT TO PREPARE BEFORE YOU NEGOTIATE

1. Prioritise what's important to you and write down what are 'must-haves' in your chosen car, compared with 'nice-to-haves'. Must-haves could be a 2-litre engine or above, diesel and power steering, whereas nice-to-have could be a GPS system, heated seats and climate control.

Must-have	Like-to-have
• power steering	• DVD player in back
• rear windscreen wiper	• GPS system
• 2.0 litre diesel engine	• leather interior
• carry five adults	• blue metallic paint
• side air bags	• alloy wheels
• air conditioning	• full tank of fuel
• family-sized boot	• climate control
• CD player	

An example of a must-have and like-to-have list.

2. Get the brochures for the various models you are interested in. List the ones that are your top two or three choices and look at the benefits each has. Benefits are personal to the individual. Some people value things like side air-bags and a more powerful engine, whereas others prefer a GPS system and individual DVD players for the children in the back of the car.

Even if you are solely set on one particular model, it may be worth having a brief look at the competition as it will help you when you negotiate. Sellers who know you have your heart set on their model have only their other own brand showrooms to compete against, and whilst this will still be an incentive, it is certainly narrowing down your options.

3. Do your research. Offers and 'special seasonal deals' are found in local and national newspapers, and range from special prices to 0% finance. You will see deals advertised across the year, but more emphasis in the UK will be around the new registration months of March and September. The adverts often appear in the months running

up to these dates, as competition for your business hots up.

Scour the internet for your dealers. Sometimes they will offer additional deals over and above the generally advertised ones. Make sure that when you compare prices, it is for a 'like-for-like' car. If they have not got a website, either call them up or visit the showroom to see if they have any special offers on at the moment.

4. Make a list of all offers and prices, and keep it with you as a reminder. By now it's likely you have already saved a fair bit of money from the original price quoted, and you haven't even negotiated yet.

5. Have in mind two prices on each car you have short-listed: the highest you are willing to pay and also your ideal price. The highest rate should really be no higher than the lowest 'like-for-like' price you have found for the model. You should consider which is more important to you: lowering the price, or getting additional extras for no more cost.

Whenever you negotiate, it is important to know your ideal outcome and your walk-away rate (see Glossary).

APPROACHING THE SHOWROOMS

Now that you have all the information to hand, you are ready to approach the showrooms. You are aware of what is key to you and the prices available, and you have an idea of what you are happy to pay.

As you enter, a good car salesman will quickly try and gain rapport with you. This is designed to make you feel welcome, comfortable and at ease.

But being relaxed in a salesperson's company can lead to you giving more away than you think, and falling into 'buying mode'. The trick is to appear off-guard and at ease even though you are actually alert and prepared!

1. Begin with the end in mind. You want to pay a good price that you are happy with. In order to do this you need to show interest but not uncontrollable excitement. You also need to make sure that the seller feels you have not made up your mind as yet and are considering a few models including ... This is where your knowledge of other possible deals from your preparation is important.

2. Prepare your opening statement with the above in mind. This can be thought of before you leave the house that day. Think about what will give them the indication that you are a genuine buyer and your custom is potentially theirs if they treat you well. An example would be:

   'Hi, I've taken today off work to find out more about my top three choices of new cars, and the Santina *is one of them. I intend to buy in the next week or so and would like to ask you a few questions if I may.*

The above indicates an intention to buy and buy soon, 'your car is up there in my list, but I'm not setting my heart on it'. A good salesman will naturally want to help.

Or, you can approach things in a different way by offering a 'delaying signal'. This could also gain you a better deal.

For example, after stating your intention to buy a new car either now or in the future, say:

   'I'm wondering whether to wait until October, as I feel the prices will be better once the 'excitement' of a new

car registration is over, and people will be saving up for Christmas instead.'

Although they know buying a car is a 'considered purchase', salespeople generally want to close the deal with you as soon as possible, since as days, weeks or months go by, you – the consumer – have more choices available, more glamorous advertising thrust upon you and potentially more important ways to use upwards of £7,000 (e.g. Christmas presents and a new kitchen). So they may offer you incentives to persuade you to buy now.

3. Prepare yourself for questions.

STEALTH TACTIC Be aware that the salesperson may want to ask you questions. Often these will help him or her to assist you in making the right choice. However, sometimes it will be to find out how keen you are to buy their model, whether a deal needs to be offered, or it is likely that you will pay the asking price.

Such questions come in numerous shapes or sizes. Examples are:

'Can I ask you where we rank in that top three?' – If you say number one, they know that you have more emotional attachment.

'What made you choose the Santina, *out of interest?'* – If you list emotional reasons, they could attempt to estimate the risk factor of you going elsewhere, which will allow them to calculate whether they have to negotiate off the full-rate in order to get your business. Equally, it **could** be to use their expertise to help you make an informed decision on the model compared with other offerings they may have.

Whenever you are asked a question, ask yourself this:

'What is their motivation for asking this?'

This will help you decide how to answer the question. If you feel it's to help **you** in your decision, then fine; if however, it's to help them to gain information about your keenness, then you may prefer not to answer, or you could try to be clever with your reply.

As an example:

'Can I ask where we rank in that top three?'

You could say:

'Currently third, but I'm prepared to be swayed!'

Another example:

'Do you want climate control?'

'Doesn't it come as standard?'

4. Listen out for the proposal. When the salesperson has got all the information they need, and you have finished asking any questions you may have, they will then quote you a rate or ask you if you want a quote. You will have a good idea of this anyway, as you will already have done your research. Make sure you go through exactly what the price includes, and that it covers all your 'must-haves'. Hopefully, some or all of your 'like-to-haves' are there, too. If not, then now is your chance to add them in.

5. Raise an objection. If not, you might as well not have bought this book! Earlier on, you would have decided what you would like to achieve from the deal. It could be a certain price, additional extras or both.

If it's price, use your research effectively. For example you could say:

'£13,000, that's a little too high, I was expecting nearer

£11,500, as I have seen offers closer to that in other showrooms.'

Or, if you would rather be less specific:

'£13,000 – that seems high, I need to have a deal that's better than that. My alternatives are cheaper. In order to get my order, are you willing to offer me a discount?'

If it's additional extras, you could say:

'£13,000, that's quite high. But if it included all the extras that I am considering, then I might be able to consider that price.'

Here you are showing interest and saying that, if your conditions are met, the price that they are offering **could** be possible.

This is where you can use your 'like-to-have' list, and see what you can add in. Try for as many as possible at first, as you can always come down.

6. Take time to consider the deal on offer. Thank the dealer for their assistance and ask them to print a quote out for you, with all the added extras. Having an offer in writing saves confusion later on, as when you come back, the salesperson may be on a day off and there will be no confirmation of the offer given. Let them know you are going to consider their proposal, and also use the rest of the day to see your other car options. It may be worth saying:

'If there are just a few hundred pounds in it, would you be willing to look again at your offer?'

A straight 'no' is the only likely answer that suggests not. If it's 'come back to me' or similar, then there is definitely a chance.

7. See your other car showrooms and apply a similar approach. Though this time you will have a concrete offer in your hands that can be used to help in your negotiation. When the price comes up, you can use this quote in your justifications to them to better their offer. For example:

'I appreciate your offer; however, I can buy a similar model at £12,200, and it has all the extras included already. Your car is one I would like to consider, but I would need it to at least .... that price.' [Add in 'match, beat or come closer to,' where applicable!]

8. Look at your options and then decide. You can of course try this a couple of times with each showroom, but judge whether you feel it necessary or indeed fruitful. You are likely to be at the final stages of a negotiation, and this is where a conditional offer (see Glossary) is really helpful to see if you can squeeze a little bit more from the deal. Here is where you use the 'if and then' approach. You could say:

*'**If** you agree to adding in a free full tank of fuel* [and/or GPS, car mats, etc.], ***then** I will buy the car off you today.'*

'If and then' is an approach that is often used in business negotiation which only commits you to a deal if they agree with the condition you have imposed upon it. In this example, the condition is fuel. They can of course say no; however, it doesn't stop you from agreeing the deal without it.

CONFIRMING YOUR DEAL

Now you have verbally confirmed the deal, it is then important to read all the paperwork to ensure price, delivery and added extras are **all** written down and confirmed in your contract. Verbal deals are not worth the paper they are **not** written on!

When buying a new car, it is likely you will wait several weeks for delivery, and a lot can change in that time, including your salesman, who may be working elsewhere. So contracts detailing everything that is not sold as 'standard' are vital.

NEGOTIATING PART EXCHANGE

Deals can also be negotiated on part exchange for your old car. The price offered can vary, so it's important you get the best deal you can.

As in all negotiations, preparation is key, so find out your vehicle's true worth before you part exchange it. Companies offering this service can be found on the web, and indications are often given within car magazines. List your three outcomes: firstly, the price you would be very happy to achieve (jot down some justifications for your proposal – see below), then a good outcome for you, and finally your bottom-line.

Justifications
• great condition (make sure it is!) • new tyres • low mileage • one careful owner – no claims • not sure whether to buy *Santina* or not, this could decide me! (Intimating you are not committed to using their showroom, and you could go elsewhere.)

Again, it is important that you don't limit your options, as if you are not happy with the part-exchange price you have been offered, you can always sell it privately. If the salesman is aware of this, it also makes them realise that you are not necessarily committed to buying a car from them.

Use the 'if and then' approach mentioned earlier in this chapter to help you get the best deal you can. For example:

You:	Showroom salesperson:
'If you can give me £6,500 part exchange for my car, then I will buy the Santina at £11,000.'	'Mmm … That's too much; however, I could give you £6,250 if you buy the Santina at £11,000, and I will throw in a tank of fuel.'

This will not commit you to the deal unless they agree with your terms. If they offer an alternative deal, it is then up to you whether you accept it or continue to bargain until you are happy.

WHAT'S IN IT FOR THEM?

Car salespeople are invariably on a bonus or commission, and it forms a significant part of their salary. Often these are monthly targets, and therefore establishing as much information as you can about how close they are to reaching their next level will help you understand their keenness to do a deal.

You may want to show an interest in their targets and casually ask how the month has been for the showroom and them in particular. Perhaps ask them whether they are targeted monthly or weekly. This may or may not give you the information you want, but it's worth a try if you feel brave!

IN SUMMARY

1. List your must-haves and nice-to haves.

2. Get all the brochures and information to help you choose.

3. Prepare yourself effectively. Do background work on your top three choices. Look at the strengths and weaknesses of each, so that you can use the information effectively depending on which showroom you are talking to. Look at the range of prices that are offered so that you are aware of what is a good or a bad deal. Remember you want to gain the best price!

4. Don't fall for the flattering sales lines that may be offered to you.

5. Emotionally, don't seem too enthusiastic about the vehicle, as this gives huge buying signals to the salesperson and will probably affect their keenness to negotiate.

6. From your preparation, use the information wisely. Raise some objections against the product that will help you gain a better price. Emphasising the benefits of their competitors may help here.

7. Remember to see if you can add in some of your 'nice-to-haves' as added extras. Use the 'if and then' approach.

8. If buying at a later date, make sure you have the offer (including the extras) in writing.

9
Buying electrical goods

In today's world, electrical goods account for an increasing proportion of your annual spend. These can include anything from the humble toaster, through fridges and cookers, to televisions, DVD players, and home cinema kits of truly beast-like proportions. This chapter will show you how to strike better deals when buying any of your household appliances, executive necessities or the latest gadget that pushes all the buttons.

THE BENEFITS OF NEGOTIATING

1. Your spend in this category will vary; however, your savings in hard cash on a television system, fridge freezer, washing machine and oven could easily amount to a combined total of over £400.

2. If you're buying a printer or DVD player, these products often aren't supplied with the leads that make them work – get them included in the price!

3. Why buy the 'package deals' on offer, when you can create your own with the items **you** want to buy?

SO WHAT DO WE CHOOSE AS EXAMPLES?

So many products to choose from ... but we will use two situations as examples.

In the first, you are looking to buy a fridge freezer – straightforward enough. In the second, we will look at negotiating package deals: in other words, persuading a given store or outlet to offer you better prices if you buy multiple products.

THE FRIDGE FREEZER

What to prepare before you negotiate

1. Size matters! Make sure it will fit into the slot you have for it – so measure up.

2. Research your product options by going round the shops, looking at brochures and trawling the internet – also, ask friends for any recommendations.

   Many stores have a website these days, so you can do your shopping virtually if you wish, though with products of high capital cost, it may be worth seeing them in the flesh (or metal as the case may be!).

   What's important to you in the fridge freezer? Energy efficiency over price? Larger freezer space than fridge space?

3. Marry all this with your budget. You're spending upwards of £300 and are looking to save at least what? 10%? Make a list of what are must-haves and like-to-haves.

Must-have	Nice-to-have
• size no more than 1800mm tall, 700mm wide and 720mm deep	• using room to maximum use (1800 × 700 × 720mm) no smaller than (1750 × 600 × 624mm)
• silver	• chilled water dispenser
• energy rating A minimum	• energy rating A+
• overall price under £475 (including delivery)	• price under £400
	• larger fridge than freezer

List of must-haves and nice-to-haves on electrical goods.

4. Whittle down your list and pick the outlets. You should end up with a list of perhaps three products, in order of preference, alongside their respective prices and the places they are available.

When it comes to price, make sure you compare like with like. Some companies include delivery in their quoted price, while others charge an extra fee (and where installation is required, possibly a further cost for this as well). It's also worth taking into acount any additional costs for taking away your old appliance, if you're replacing something. Also, look for advertisements of special offers which may give you a better price or added value.

Be aware that stores often encourage you to buy on-line, and the product may be cheaper if you take this option. But also bear in mind that it is much easier to negotiate with someone face-to-face than it is on the internet, so don't discount the shops just because their prices appear slightly higher. Some shops also offer a better price if you order it on-line first for store pick-up later, so always be aware of the on-line price even if you are planning to negotiate face-to-face.

FF1	FF2	FF3

• covers all must-haves
• size
  1800 × 700 × 710
• chilled water dispenser
• energy A rating
	• covers all must-haves
	• size
	  1795 × 690 × 700
	• chilled water dispenser
	• energy A+ rating
		• covers all must-haves
		• size
		  1750 × 600 × 624
		• energy A rating

• internet £430 inc. delivery • store A £430 not including delivery (additional £15) • store B £450 including delivery • store C £475 including delivery	• internet £440 inc. delivery • store A £440 not including delivery (additional £15) • store B £450 including delivery • store C £495 including delivery	• internet special offer £345 inc. delivery (normally £375) • store A £375 including delivery • store B £385 including delivery

Specifications of fridge freezers and prices on offer.

5. List your fridge freezers in order of preference. What's important to you? For example, is it price over size, or energy efficiency over price? In this case, we will plump for FF1: although its energy rating is only A, the size makes the biggest use of the space available and the price is slightly cheaper than FF2. However, although I've selected these criteria as the key ones for this, there's nothing to stop you building up a similar case using, say, energy efficiency as your number one goal.

6. Prepare the points that will help you get a good price for FF1. You have done some good groundwork on three products, so you can use a lot of this information to help you. It has probably helped you to save a certain amount already, by not relying on the first store that you saw the product in, and doing a little digging. I have often managed

to save around 10% at this stage, and on a £450 product, that's already £45. Let's look at the facts:

a. Your third choice product costs as little as £345 (Store A has it for £375), and would be acceptable to you.

b. FF2 has a higher energy rating (A+), and this appeals to
. a lot of people. It is both slightly smaller and more expensive than FF1.

c. FF1 can be bought for as little as £430 (although Store C has it for £475), has an energy rating that's acceptable to you and a size that's near perfect.

Use this information to plan your conversation. Either write it down, or get it very clear in your head – practise if possible.

The negotiation

Have in mind the price you would ideally pay for FF1 (in this case £390 without delivery, or £395 with delivery), and a walk-away rate (£420 not including delivery, or £425). In this case you have a BATNA (see Glossary) in FF2 or FF3, and you have several stores and opportunities to negotiate these if required!

Also assume (at this stage anyway) that Store C is too expensive, and approach Store B. Using the information you have acquired, a conversation could go along these lines:

You: 'Over the next couple of weeks I am looking to replace my fridge freezer. I was interested in FF3 as it was within my price range	This is a statement of intent: you are not saying you are desperate to buy (these products can often be urgent purchases if the previous one has broken!). Therefore, the salesperson knows you have choice. Secondly, you are implying that £345 is your budget, but with a little persuasion and incentive, you may be sold the idea of a more expensive product.

at £345. However, in your store it's £385. Perhaps I can look at FF1, if I am to pay around the £385 level.'	You are also letting them know you have done your homework and can buy cheaper elsewhere.
Salesperson: '£345, where did you see that?'	The salesperson could be testing the authenticity of your claim: perhaps a price promise is a guarantee of the store (when a shop guarantees to at least match the price of their competitors – though often these are within a certain radius and do not include internet prices).
You: 'On the internet, and including delivery as well. However, if you offered FF1 for £385, including delivery then I'd consider that.'	I would suggest not going for the kill quite yet, i.e. saying you would buy it now, as this may give them the idea that you are not too well versed in negotiation and intended to buy now anyway!
Salesperson: 'No, £385 is too cheap/not an option [OR] no the retail price for that is £450, I can't possibly do it for that.'	Listen for what is **not** said. 'Too cheap' or 'can't do it for that' indicates a possible deal here, as it is not saying they will not trade.
You: 'That's a shame. If I was to look to buy that one in the next few weeks, what price could you offer me?'	You **could** go for the kill (if so, go down two lines), but in this case, you are not yet committing to the deal **now**, which is what they would be interested in.
Salesperson: 'Well, prices vary from day to day; are you in a position to buy now?'	
You: 'Mmmm, possibly. If the deal was right, maybe I could bring it forward.'	
Salesperson: 'If you were to buy today, I could knock 10% off the price.'	Making it £405 plus delivery.

You: 'So £405 including delivery.'	What I call an assumptive close, where you put something in 'assuming' it's included in the deal. In which case they have to say 'no' to take it out.
Salesperson: 'Ahh, the £405 was not including delivery. With delivery it would normally be a further £15, but we will do it for £410.'	Still a good saving on delivery charges.
You: 'That's still over my budget.'	
Salesperson: 'What's your budget?'	Fair enough to ask – up to you if you tell them a figure. I do suggest being a little conservative if you do!
You: 'Put it this way, a fraction under £400.'	
Salesperson: 'I can't do that I'm afraid.'	As it is only £10.01 away from 'under £400', this could be genuine (or there may be a 'higher' decision-maker who can help here). At this stage, if you can consider it for a day or even an hour, this gives the option of talking to other stores (but if the saving is going to be tiny and you have to pay more in petrol to get to another store, you may want to take the deal, otherwise it's a false economy) – ask for some time to consider (get them to agree to this and make sure you have their name).

Now you have a price commitment of £410, you can happily go to Store A to negotiate.

Conversation with Store A

You: *'I'm interested in FF1, and, although initially I was considering buying in a couple of months, Store B has persuaded me to think of buying now, as they offered me a great deal. You started off cheaper, but now are more expensive. If I buy now, could you beat their price?'*	Store B have already said they won't go under £410. You haven't told Store A the price. To me this seems less aggressive. You are giving Store A the opportunity to either decline getting into a price war with their competitor and accept they won't get the business, or take the opportunity of competing with them.
Salesperson: *'Possibly, what have they offered you?'*	Non-commital answer, but interested.
You: *'£410 including delivery.'*	
Salesperson: *'That's a good offer, what would make you buy now?'*	Good question from a salesperson. No point in offering you something for you to say no. They have also acknowledged you have already been given a great offer.
You: *'If you agree to £385, then I will buy now.'*	Pushing it a bit further than you would accept – why not?
Salesperson: *'That's too cheap . If I were to offer it to you for £395, would you accept?'*	There you go, £35 cheaper than anywhere, and probably a lot cheaper than the first price you saw the fridge freezer advertised for!

As with many electrical goods, you will be asked if you want to take out their insurance. I am not getting involved in the 'do or don't' of this; however, if you do take it out, remember that the price is often negotiable, too!

Using this for all electrical goods

The above example can be applied to many electrical goods. Whether you are buying an MP3 player or the mother of all home cinema systems, similar theories and practices apply. As a rule of thumb, I always balance the amount of time spent on preparing your case with the potential money saved. Saving £5? Then spend the appropriate time on it. If there are potential savings of £250, more detail will probably pay dividends. Preparation will save you money and potentially help you choose a better product, so it is a great exercise to go through anyway.

Over time, you will find that saving £5 or £10 is easy, as often it's just a matter of a quick look at some offers and speaking politely and confidently to a salesperson to get what you want.

PACKAGING

There is nothing more appealing to a salesperson than someone coming in with wads of cash, saying: 'Please look after me, I am happy to spend, spend, spend!'

Packaging is very prevalent in business, and allows all parties to benefit from a deal. Often, both in business and the retail world, it is driven by the salesperson. Advertisements encourage you to bulk purchase, with offers of three for two, or a computer deal that includes printer and paper. But why not create your own packages, tailored to your needs? Maybe you have a printer, but need a computer, digital camera, DVD recorder and television – and would like SCART leads, DVD-rewriters and a memory card for your camera. So let's use that as an example.

Not all stores will have the various products and brands – the bigger and more diverse the package is, the more likely it is that you will be limited to larger stores or specialist shops.

Calculators at the ready

A mathematical mind would be handy when it comes to packaging, although reading what to do is much more complicated than actually doing it. Where possible, I have tried to explain the sums so that they can be followed more easily. A calculator will certainly help!

What to prepare before you negotiate

1. What is it you want? Often, if you can wait a while to build up your shopping list of electrical goods, you can get some great deals. The more you have to offer a retailer, the better the deal is likely to be. List the products you need/want (nice-to-haves and must-haves). We are going to assume that all of these products can be bought under one roof.

Must-have	Nice-to-have
• television	•SCART leads
• computer	• DVD RWs
• DVD recorder	• 1GB SD memory card
• digital camera	

List of must-haves and nice-to-haves for your package deal.

2. Research the products you want. Use the internet, brochures, advertisements, and browsing the shops to get the details of the products and the various prices you can get (see page 131 for how you should detail each product's specifications and decide your preferences).

3. Table the prices, one for individual products and one for store packages. This will allow you to see what the best individual prices are, alongside the best package offers the stores can make.

List alternative products if you are prepared to have them. I would only do this for the main items and not the peripherals (SCART leads, etc.) as the prices of these account for only a small percentage of the overall package.

Store and individual products and pricing

Television	Computer
Store A TV1: £899	Store A PC1: £499
Store B TV1: £899	Store B PC1: £530
Store C TV1: £899	Store C PC1: £489
Internet TV1: £839	
Digital Camera	**DVD recorder**
Store A Cam1: £199	Store A DVD1: £199
Store B Cam1: £179	Store B DVD1: £199
Store C Cam1: £185	Store C DVD1: £175 (special
Internet Cam1: £157	offer for month only)
	Internet DVD1: £175

Package prices for stores

Store A	Total package price: £1,796
Store B	Total package price £1,807
Store C	Total package price: £1,748 **Best in-store package**
Purchasing off the internet computer not available	£1,171 If you bought the computer from Store C, this would make the package price £1,660

So, you can see that trading over the internet will already save you £88 if you buy everything except the computer in this way – and obtain the PC from Store C. But there is a good chance that you can save more than this if you negotiate face-to-face. If not, then you can always go back to the internet.

4. What price are you happy to pay? List two or three outcomes.

Ideal	Good	Walk-away
£1,550	£1,600	£1,650 (you know £1,660 is already possible via the internet and buying the computer from Store C).

You would also consider more than £1,650, if you were given free added value (e.g. SCART leads, DVD RW, etc.).

5. Let's look at the facts.

A. In two out of four cases, the internet offers better prices.

B. Store C matches the internet (for only a month) on the DVD recorder and offers the cheapest price for the PC.

C. Store B has the cheapest digital camera (bar the internet).

Now let's use these facts!

The negotiation

Let's assume the decision is between A and C for the moment, as they offer the best package prices. In this instance, start with Store A, as although Store C has a better price, you can always revert to it if Store A won't discount enough – giving you two bites of the cherry. Use the facts and prices shown earlier to create your strategy. A conversation could go like this:

You: *'I'm interested in buying a television and computer over the next few weeks, and I see you have TV1 and PC1. If I was to buy both from you, what deal would you be able to offer me?'*	Notice that you haven't laid everything on the table straight away. It's good to show that you want a package deal, but you can gain further discounts if you add more things in later (especially if these come up with seamless logic: in this case, a camera as an addition to your PC, and a DVD recorder for your television). Also, you haven't asked: 'what's your best deal?' as this can back the salesperson into a corner and make them reluctant to increase the discount initially offered.
Salesperson: *'Are you in a position to buy now?'*	
You: *'Well, possibly, if the deal was right.'*	Non-commital, but showing that you may be interested at the right price.
Salesperson: *'OK, if you were to buy both now, we would do them both for £1,300.'*	Full price £1,398 (discount of approximately 7% off Store A price)
You: *'Well, I can buy TV1 for £839 and PC1 for £489 elsewhere, in which case your discount only amounts to £28. I would need more of an incentive.'*	Putting your preparation information to good use! It's possible you will be asked where those better deals are from, as, when comparing prices, shops tend to measure themselves against a particular competitor, rather than picking prices from many outlets. But it shouldn't matter, as it's

	about what you can buy cheaper elsewhere, and the store that doesn't listen to this will probably lose out on this deal. So, assuming you get over that hurdle …
Salesperson: *'OK, how about £1,260?'*	Approximately 10% off Store A price
You: *'I appreciate the discount; however, it's still only £68 off what I can buy elsewhere. It may be worth me waiting a while for prices to come down. I am thinking of buying a couple of extra items over the next few months — could this help reduce the overall price?'*	Now you've added them in when the deal seems quite close. More products could mean theoretically a better deal! They may click that you had this in mind all the time, but you never said you didn't!
Salesperson: *'What else are you thinking of?'*	
You: *'I am looking to perhaps buy a camera and a DVD recorder.'*	Guide them in the direction of the ones you wanted, although it may at this stage be worth saying you are considering a few and look at these others as well.
Salesperson: *'Well, for all of this, if you buy now, we will offer you £1,600.'*	£196 (c11%). The next step is if you wanted to give it that extra push!
You: *'I appreciate that, though that means that you are charging me £340 for the DVD recorder and camera, and I can buy these for £332 elsewhere. Is there any further incentive you could give, be it money or free add-ons for the products I am buying?'*	
Salesperson: *'Well, that's all I can do on the money, but I could throw in a SCART lead, if that will secure the deal.'*	Now a choice. Do you want to close a deal with an 'if and then'? For example: 'If you also add in a pack of DVD rewriters and a 1GB SD memory card, then I will buy all that now.' Or alternatively, buy yourself some time. Then read on …

You: *'I appreciate that. It's a big decision. Can you give me an hour to think about it? If I'm back by four, then obviously it's a yes?'*	Now often, if they have been helpful, I would give them the opportunity to have the business and say to them: 'If I am not prepared to pay that much, is it worth me coming back to discuss it further?' You are being fair.

Now on to Store C. If the stores are more than a walk apart, you can always take a number to ring them on and let them know your decision.

Are you giving Store C a chance?

If so, then approach with the same politeness and courtesy. You can either decide to go through the whole scenario as above, or cut to the chase and tell them what needs to be done – without sounding threatening – no one likes being given ultimatums.

A conversation could go along these lines:

> *'I am in a position to buy today. A competitor has offered me a great deal on the following items* [list them]. *Will you be willing to discuss a package deal?'*

If the answer is yes, they are likely to ask what the price was.

If they offer a better deal (perhaps with price or increasing the package offering), it is fair to ask:

> *'Is that the best offer you are willing to make?'*

If the answer comes back firmly 'yes', then you know where you stand. If they say something like: 'come back to us', it is likely they will go further.

If you have given your promise to Store A, then you should honour it (you may even get a better deal!). Now it is likely you will be talking pounds and pence, and you have to weigh up the profitability of going to and fro and using up your time (although you may be having a bit of fun with it!).

IN SUMMARY

1. Spend time researching both the products and the outlets available to you. This has two benefits: firstly, you may find a better product than you originally thought; and secondly, it's likely you will find it cheaper the harder you look (until you become a professional in seeking the bargains!).

2. List the must-haves and nice-to-haves with your products/packages. Put in order your preferred purchases.

3. List two or three outcomes: ideal, good and walk-away packages/prices.

4. Use the prepared information to your advantage. Quote the lowest of prices, and be conservative with informing them of your budgets.

5. If packaging, initially talk about fewer items than you intend to buy (where possible), as it's likely a better deal will be offered when you add more.

10
How to complain effectively

SETTING THE SCENE

A couple staying in a hotel, sitting in their room one evening.

Amanda: *I'm fed up with this place. We are trying to watch television, and this Spanish film looks as if it was shot in a snow-drift. Can't they plug in their aerial properly?*

Steve: *Yes, and there was that meal too: cold and tasteless apart from the extra kick imparted by the hairs in the moussaka!*

Amanda: *Well, my food was just about OK, but the wine was pretty vinegary.*

Steve: *I know we didn't pay absolutely top dollar for this room, but you do expect a minimum of ...*

Amanda: *What I'd really like right now is a cup of coffee – and all there is on the refreshment tray is one lousy teabag. It's rubbish.*

After a restless night on a lumpy mattress, the couple rise, share the one teabag, shower in lukewarm water, get dressed and make their way down to reception. After waiting to be served for ten minutes, they are finally greeted by the receptionist.

Amanda: *We'd like to settle our bill.*

Receptionist: *Was everything to your satisfaction?*

Amanda: *Yes, it was OK, thanks.*

Receptionist: *Excellent. Would you like to pay by the credit card you gave us?*

ASSESSING THE ABOVE

Does it sound familiar? I bet it does.

This is an example of a classic British disease: moaning, but not doing anything about it.

When I began to negotiate in business, I soon realised that this was pointless. Moaning to your colleagues, your partner or your friends gets you nowhere, since they can sympathise but cannot change the situation. When you are unhappy with a product or service, you need to learn how to complain effectively to a decision-maker in order to rectify what has gone wrong, or to receive compensation. To do this you need to tell people what you want, so that they can resolve the problem.

Outside work, I have used this in many areas of life, ranging from queries over my phone bills to the price of my gym membership. As a result, I have gained good and fair deals: some of these have involved hard cash; others have involved goods or additional benefits.

Businesses want your custom, and the better ones want to hear your genuine grievances (and often have departments specially set up for this). It is well known that the best advert for a company is the praise of its customers. If you, as a consumer, extol the virtues of a particular business and the quality of its goods and customer services, you will often persuade others to try them.

As long as a complaint is approached in the right way, it can be of huge benefit to you. Let's start by looking at the above example. What Amanda and Steve should have done was:

1. Put it right straight away. If something is wrong, say so at the time. The wine was vinegary, the moussaka had hair in it – send them back. The television was not working properly, and there was no coffee or milk (and a lack of teabags!) – ring reception and sort it out.

2. When you come to the paying point, make sure you summarise all that was wrong, and then **tell** them what you want in return. For example: a free night's stay, £25 off the bill – or better still, both!

When you pay for something, you expect to get what you paid for. If you haven't, you should ask for something in return – money back or compensation, whether financial or otherwise. In fairness to a lot of companies, they are all too willing to oblige **if** they are asked.

SO WHAT IS EFFECTIVE COMPLAINING?

Effective complaining is when you are not happy with something and you take action that compensates you, or gives you assurance that something will be put in place to improve a product or service.

It can only be done if you address the situation with people who can instigate change.

SO WHERE CAN YOU DO IT?

Anywhere you are not happy with the product or service you have received such as: holidays, hotels, at an electrical store, health spas, restaurants or your internet grocery shop.

PREPARING YOUR CASE

1. Make a list of the things that are not right with your product or service. Prioritise them in order, starting with the bigger issues to you. See below for two examples.

Phone and broadband company	Hotel stay
• billed for calls and services not received	• TV not working properly when watching film
• emailed company – they said I would get a response in 48 hours but it took five days	• no coffee and milk in room
	• food cold and hair in it
• then said they would ring 9–10 am Tuesday – never phoned	• wine tasted awful

2. Examine the points above and look at why they had an impact that adversely affected you. For example, if someone arranged to call you at a specific time and they failed to – did you miss an appointment that could have led to some paid-for work?

The examples above have implications for you in terms of both money and inconvenience. Financial implications are the costs for a potential loss of earnings for the appointment. As for inconvenience – well, it is hard to put an exact figure on the value of this, but you should still be compensated.

Phone and broadband	• actual amount owed £8.50 • inconvenience for chasing email and loss of earnings c.£50 • total £58.50 (ideal) • must-have £8.50
Hotel	• actual loss – zero • disappointment and inconvenience – no coffee and milk, poor television reception, poor food and wine and overall disappointment on break away – either £35 or a free night's accommodation

PUTTING YOUR CASE

As in any negotiation, you have your 'must-haves', i.e. the money lost due to the problem, and the 'like-to-haves', which in these cases could be compensation for inconvenience and disappointment or, for example, a free meal.

Write down your ideal compensation/remuneration and your 'must-haves' along with the reasons why, and have them with you to construct your rationale.

CHOOSE YOUR FORM OF COMPLAINT

Sometimes you have no choice; however, if you do, it is likely to be either by email, phone, letter or face-to-face. All of these have benefits – but in terms of reading people's reaction, a face-to-face meeting tends to give you a better idea of what the real meaning behind their message is (see Chapter 3 on the language of negotiation) which helps you to see whether they are prepared to offer more.

Whichever route you choose, be sure to have clear in your mind what you want to achieve and why.

It is also important to prepare your opening statement. What you say first, along with your demands, are usually the things that determine what you achieve.

CONSTRUCTION OF COMPLAINT

Begin with the end result in mind. You want justice and a solution that's acceptable to you. The tone needs to be serious, but polite; the content to be succinct, have impact, be justifiable **and** offering a solution (or making a proposal) **not** just moaning about what's wrong.

If you send a letter or email – make sure it is sent to someone who can resolve your problem.

An example letter of complaint for an internet phone

Dear Sir or Madam

Re: ZP300 Internet phone

Your promised delivery of the above phone was not met (meant to be Feb 10); eventually it was delivered ten days late. However, it arrived damaged and I returned it immediately, incurring costs of £2.50 post and packaging. The replacement arrived seven days later, but was not the colour I ordered.

This service is not what I would, or indeed should accept from a reputable company like yours. It meant that I had to make calls on my landline during that period, costing me £15.21 plus £5 line rental. The phone was not the colour I ordered, but I will accept the one you have sent, rather than incur another £2.50 and a further delay.

I would like a total of £35 compensation for costs incurred, the inconvenience suffered because of your delays, and the fact that the product supplied was not the one I ordered.

I look forward to receiving your response, along with reimbursement, so that I can close the matter, reassured that customer care is important to you, and you have paid attention to my genuine complaints.

Yours faithfully
………

The above letter is formal, states the facts, costs incurred and inconvenience factor, and has an 'assumptive close' (see Glossary) that assumes they will meet the terms laid out, in return for closing the matter satisfactorily. Both emails and letters are good for stating facts; however, make sure to eliminate any ambiguity or words or phrases that could be taken different ways, as this is the weakness of this type of communication.

ON THE PHONE

Make sure you are speaking to somebody who is able to resolve your issues, i.e. a decision-maker. If in doubt, ask.

Steve: *'Good morning. I wish to make a complaint. Are you the person I need to speak to?'*

Customer care team: *'Yes sir, my name is Rick, how may I help?'*

Steve: *'Hello Rick, my name is Steve. My wife and I recently returned from a holiday with your company in Malaga. The holiday we booked with you was for seven nights' accommodation in Hotel de Lux with sea view.*

However, when we arrived, we were told that we would be going to Hotel Grots Ville as there was no room in our chosen accommodation.

Despite this being another 4-star hotel, it was not what we had booked and was an extremely disappointing alternative.

The rooms were small and badly kept; I have pictures I can send you. The hotel was 15 minutes from the beach and the room obviously did not offer a sea view.

This was totally unacceptable to us as the accommodation was not what we had booked, and was in our opinion below the standard of our chosen hotel. To this end we believe that we should be refunded £250 as compensation for this.'

Rick: *'Well sir, I am sorry that you had a disappointing experience with us and can fully understand your frustration. I can appreciate that you would like to be compensated for this; however, £250 is over a quarter of the ...'*

And then the negotiation begins! (See Chapter 2 for a general negotiation overview.)

This example carries significant weight as you have pictures that prove your point. Also, make sure you make a note of the time, date and person you speak to.

FACE-TO-FACE

Face-to-face complaints have their advantages, and if you are returning goods (except of course by post), it's often the only way.

Although you may feel uncomfortable with face-to-face complaints, it is fair to say that so does the recipient – well, most of the time anyway!

Emotional disappointment often comes over with greater strength in such a situation. So, if you explain your position verbally, visually and emotionally, in an effective way, you will stand a greater chance of success.

Again, it's advantageous to prepare an opening statement and what you want to get out of it (two solutions – one ideal and one acceptable).

STEALTH TACTIC There is no harm in discussing your complaint in public view, in a polite but confident manner, as this can act as an excellent catalyst to its being resolved!

A BRIEF NOTE ON COMPLAINING IN A RESTAURANT

All this applies to any form of complaint; however, when you are dealing with a restaurant, it is important to remember that someone has personally prepared something for you. With this in mind, make sure that their feelings are handled carefully, as politeness and sensitivity will go a long way!

This is especially true if you are sending something back to be re-heated, cooked more or changed – upset someone at this stage at your peril!

Think of how you would want to be treated. An example of sensitivity could be:

'The steak tastes wonderful; however, I love my fries really crispy, that's a personal taste. Could you give them five more minutes please? Many thanks.'

IN SUMMARY

1. Do not moan or, worse still, say nothing. Take action and let people know what's wrong. Provide evidence if you have some.

2. Tell them what you want. Offer your solution, be it compensation, money off, or a free product.

3. Always be polite but firm. Often you are dealing with departments that handle 'moaning' and complaints all day. A polite customer who offers solutions will have more chance of getting what they want.

4. Sensitivity prevails where food is concerned!

SECTION C

WORK-RELATED
NEGOTIATIONS

This part of the book is deliberately set apart from the rest.

This is because work-related negotiations have significantly more bearing on relationships than any other negotiation mentioned previously. The end result is no longer to get a deal and use tactics in order to get it. An employee's relationship with an employer needs to be developed positively in an atmosphere of trust and teamwork, and any negotiation has to be done with this in mind.

11
Getting better pay conditions

SETTING THE SCENE

It's 3.45 pm on a Friday, as Alex stumbles out of the 16th floor lift of Budgie Wharf and feels that since he has six pints of bravery inside him, now is the right time to knock on his manager Katie's door and iron out an issue that has been on his mind for the last three weeks.

Alex: *'Hi Katie, I want to broach the subject of pay. I know there's never a good time, but I really feel I should have an increase.'*

Katie: *'OK Alex, why don't we diarise some time next week to discuss things fully?'*

Alex: *'Well, if it's OK with you, I would like to strike whilst the iron's hot and do it now.'*

Katie: *'OK, if that's what you prefer, take a seat. Did you have a nice lunch?'*

Alex: *'Yes thanks, had a few beers with an old mate, and, you know how it is, we got chatting and before I knew it, six pints later and I'm running back to my desk not realising the time!'*

Katie: *'Yes, well, you're here now. How can I help?'*

Alex: *'Well, Katie – Sally and I have just bought a new house and the mortgage is crippling me, which means that an exotic holiday is out this year, and you know how Sally loves her holidays! I need to earn more money and I heard Jack gets paid £4,000 more than me. This seems a bit excessive, especially considering he is constantly phoning his girlfriend in Auckland, using the company's phone. I know he's your favourite and all, but if you can see your way to paying me an extra £4,000, I'll be really grateful.'*

ASSESSING THE ABOVE

I have visions of you cowering behind the sofa at this stage, thinking there is no way on earth any sane, sensible individual would take such action. In fairness, I have exaggerated this to make a point, but it is easy to make unfortunate errors in our bid to get the sensitive subject of pay-rises off our chest, thinking that a 'brave moment' is the appropriate time. In reality, a well-prepared moment is invariably the right time.

1. Judge the best way to communicate effectively with your boss. If your manager is the type who dislikes things coming up in casual conversation, then arrange a meeting to discuss such matters.

2. Relentlessly prepare your justifications and don't rely upon your gift of the gab.

3. Make sure your behaviour and work input befits a pay-rise. If you want to gain an increase, ensure that you have good grounds to do so. This chapter is to help you negotiate

when there is adequate justification, and is not about helping you sell ice-cubes to Eskimos!

4. Showing an employer the benefits they do and will get from you, and why you deserve an increase, is what will persuade them. Do not give justifications that look at what you need or want to spend the rise on. Show them what they are going to gain by investing in you.

5. Oh yes ... preferably not done after a few drinks!

THE TYPES OF PAY NEGOTIATIONS

We will discuss two types of negotiation.

1. An improved package: both in terms of a pay increase, and something that involves personal development.

2. A pay negotiation when you are offered a new job.

IMPROVED PACKAGE FOR A CURRENT ROLE

Although it would be nice to know that, whenever you deserve a pay-rise, your boss would automatically call you in and give it you without the need to ever darken his or her door, this is not always the case. Sometimes you need to make the choice as to whether to get on with life being underpaid; try and find a new job and then use it to persuade your current employers to increase your package; or take the bull by the horns, and go in and ask for a rise.

As a consummate optimist, I am going to assume we are going for the last option.

Try and create the best, most comprehensive reasons that you can give your boss, which will leave him or her with the thought that 'of course we should give Alex more, and we are happy to do so'. This is assuming it is within their power. If not, then you need to raise the issue with the person who can make the decision, and that can mean higher than your line manager.

PREPARING YOUR CASE

1. Research similar jobs/positions both within the company and externally, and, if possible, see how much people are remunerated for their role. Look at conditions as well as actual pay. Although internal information is useful, openly using the salary comparisons as justifications can have negative results. So, if it's available to you, be aware of the information, even if only for your own yardstick of what's possible.

   A package comparison of similar roles outside your current company often gives you an acceptable objective benchmark to discuss, but whether you use this should depend on the kind of boss you are dealing with (see 'understanding your manager' later in the chapter).

   For positions outside your organisation, get an idea of the feel of the place and what it's like to work there – you never know, you could like it so much you may decide to apply for a position with them instead.

Sally – paid £34k. Same benefits although joined two years earlier, and at that time they offered six weeks' holiday after three years' service. Is not involved in mentoring.	**Steve** – started at roughly the same time. Paid between £33 and £37k. Same benefits. No extra roles.

Me – worked for company for three years. £31k, car and pension, subsidised gym membership, five weeks' holiday and working hours 9 – 5 with a one hour lunch break.

John – paid £30k though is a junior. Same benefits and also on a sales course paid for by the company.	**Jessica** – salary unknown. Same benefits though.

Internal information gathered. For your eyes only!

Company A
- pay between £35,000 and £38,000
- hours 9 – 5.30, 1.5 hours lunch break
- company pension and car
- five weeks' holiday per year, after five years an extra week
- 'Great people to work for. Really listen to their staff and believe in investing in your development. I wouldn't work for anyone else.'

Company B
- pay between £33,000 and £36,000
- hours 9 – 5, one hour lunch break
- company pension and car
- five weeks' holiday, then six weeks' holiday after two years
- leave one hour early on a Friday between May and September
- 'Nice company. I'm not a career person, but that doesn't seem to matter. They have a high turnover of staff.'

> **Company C**
> - pay between £33,000 and £35,000
> - hours 9 – 5, one hour break
> - company pension
> - five weeks' holiday, then six weeks after two years
> - 'Love working here. I regard it as part of my social life. People are fun, but I wouldn't stay if money was priority to me.'

External information gathered for people with similar roles.

2. Think of your reason for why you believe that you deserve a pay increase. Is it because there are people who do similar roles who are paid more than you? Are you out-performing everyone on your level, and feel your pay should reflect that? If so, what specifically are you doing that makes you more valuable? Are you taking on more responsibility or work and your remuneration is not reflecting that? Are similar roles in other organisations paid more than you? Remember that one way of looking at remuneration involves pay and performance being linked. Therefore is there a possibility you could suggest a measurable bonus structure, that will help you to achieve an increase if you outperform your current levels? If there is no particular reason with your current responsibilities, is there anything you would like (or be prepared) to add into the role that would benefit both your development and also the company? Agreeing to take on added responsibility can help to gain an improved package.

If it's a significant development qualification like an MBA that you are after, again think of why you deserve to be considered. Are you keen to develop your career with this company? Have you a reputation for being studious and focused? Are there schemes within the company already set up? Are there any other companies, within your industry, sponsoring their employees to do MBAs? Also think of how the company will benefit from sponsoring you for this course; will they be able to see physical benefits from investing in you? Can you use your learning to develop the company and individuals within it? What returns can they expect? Are there any case studies (either internally or externally) that can prove how a company has benefited from sending people on these courses? How can you assure them that you will use this to benefit the company rather than going to work for somebody else?

Team get paid between £33k and £37k for same job. Sally has extra week's holiday.
Industry standard seems to be £33–£38k. Additional benefits as well.
Additionally to the job I mentor two new staff.

Summary of key information gleaned from external and internal departments compared with your current role.

3. Prepare your request for a meeting. Why leave anything to chance? The right introduction to this type of conversation can really lay the foundations for a positive, and hopefully, fruitful meeting. You want the boss to realise the subject you want to discuss, so that they can be adequately prepared and, importantly, not feel like they are being threatened or caught off-guard.

    Regardless of what people say, there is no one answer to how to approach the boss. It depends on their personality and mindset towards communication in business. Understanding your manager will help here.

Understanding your manager

The advantage of an internal negotiation in an existing role is that it is more likely you will have an understanding of your boss before you discuss a pay rise with them. It is an important element of business that you know how to manage upwards.

A. Understanding their current workload/challenges. Picking the right moment is extremely important. Hassled and stressed looks, following a particularly tough board meeting, suggest that a more appropriate moment may be later! It's also important not to leave the discussion until the last moment, as you could be stepping into an unreasonable and unfruitful meeting because of its late timing.

B. Understanding your manager's style. Are they brutally direct? If so, do they value that from their employees? Do they like preparing relentlessly and not being caught off-guard? Do they like to be relaxed (and discussing the idea via enjoyment, for example, breakfast?). Do they like humour, or a serious face-to-face discussion? Give some thought to this beforehand – the better you understand their style, the more likely you are to create the right atmosphere.

C. Know what's important to them. Are they company-focused? Do they feel that you should regard it as an honour to work for the company, no matter what the wage? Or are they people-focused, understanding the needs of the individual, and believing that if you work hard you should be rewarded for it? Are they a combination of these? Are they a listener, valuing good staff and wanting to keep them? Or are they a 'no-one's indispensible' manager, who

164

feels that if you were to go tomorrow, a replacement would be sitting at your desk within minutes. Understanding what they value will allow you to discuss your proposal in the most effective manner.

Examples of top-line profiling

Current work-load of boss: Heavy, diary is busy (with external and internal meetings). This week she has the board meeting and seems preoccupied. Department is currently stretched and is working on projects that were meant to be completed two weeks ago.

Katie's style:

Likes	Dislikes
direct approach	skirting around subjects
face-to-face contact	whingers and moaners
time to prepare	being put on the spot

Possible opening statement:

'Hi Katie. I understand you're busy at the moment; I'm manic on the Butler project as well. However, I would like to catch up with you soon. Could I put half an hour in your diary, either next week or the week after, to discuss ideas and thoughts regarding the department, my role and contribution, and also get some feedback from you?'

Current work-load of boss: Busy, but not hectic. Budgets are in, and they seem happy that that's out of the way.

Katie's style:

Likes	Dislikes
non-confrontation	direct approach
work-hard, play-hard mentality	formal meetings
being sociable	threats

Possible opening statement:

'Hi Katie. I saw in your diary you are free on the 12th first thing in the morning [before work hours]. *In return for discussing my role, contribution and ideas I have for the department, can I buy you some breakfast at the Garden Hotel?'*

In both examples, an outline of the meeting is given, an indication that it is a two-way discussion, an element of 'what's in it for them', whilst using the information about understanding your manager to positive effect. Both examples are set out deliberately not to give an impression of 'I want ...', nor any demands.

Also, the words 'pay increase' are not there, being replaced by 'role and contribution'. My personal opinion is that pay is a sensitive subject and should be treated accordingly and put into context with justifications and rationale. This cannot be communicated in 20 seconds (if it can, you may want to rethink your pitch!). If you feel more comfortable, then maybe use the word 'remuneration', directly telling them the exact subject.

Be prepared to be quizzed at this stage – it may not happen, but always be a step ahead! As an example:

Katie: *'Sure, is there anything in particular you want to discuss?'*

Alex: *'Several things, including ideas I have, remuneration and your opinions and thoughts for the coming year.'*

I call this the 'wage sandwich'. Your key issue (i.e. the main ingredient!), and the side bits, top and tailing it (the bread!).

Again, this example is dependent upon your thoughts and understanding of how your boss reacts positively, as some may prefer a more direct approach.

4. Know what you want: having a clear understanding of what you want to achieve, as well as what you are happy to accept, is important. Maybe it's not just financial additions. I have separated out two types of increase: firstly, a financial rise, and then, secondly, a personal development element (in this case, studying for a part-time MBA, and having the company sponsor you). This has significant value both financially (an MBA often costs over £10,000) and also in personal development terms.

In both examples, I would suggest three outcomes; ideal, i.e. your best outcome (assuming you are not leaving the proposal to them); a good outcome, a happy compromise; finally, acceptable, really the lowest you are happy to accept, still feeling valued and listened to.

Ideal	Good	Acceptable
• £35,500 (+14.5%)	• £34,000 (+9.7%)	• £32,750 (+5.6%)

Looking at three outcomes for remuneration package.

Ideal	Good	Acceptable
• paid-for MBA • extra ten days to attend course days	• paid-for MBA • extra five days to attend course days	• 50% paid-for MBA • extra five days to attend course days

Looking at three outcomes for development package.

5. Prepare the benefits to the employer, i.e. what's in it for them. It's all well and good to know what you want and why **you** want it; however, that is looking at it from your perspective, and doesn't normally do much for persuading the employer. They need to see what value it will gain them and/or the company. The good news about doing your justifications for the ideal outcome is that they rarely change for good and acceptable: therefore, effective preparation at the start will really pay dividends.

£35,500

- been a loyal employee for three years
- salaries in other companies average around £35,000 for similar roles
- in addition to that role, I mentor two people
- consistently in the top three salespeople within our department
- increased my clients' business by 15% year on year (compared with a departmental average of +1%)
- I know we are employing two more people, and in return for you increasing my salary, I am happy to take on more responsibility by mentoring one of them
- (know but not say) all are on more money –Sally £3,000 and Stephen between £2,000 and £6,000 more

An example of 'what's in it for the company/boss' justification for a pay-rise.

paid-for MBA	extra ten days to attend course
• Although it will benefit me, the company will also benefit hugely from the outcomes, as I will learn so much that will help the business. (Examples of subjects: marketing, finance, HR and management skills.) • Will allow me to use the course to give development ideas to the company. Happy to offer a quarterly meeting to discuss the outcomes. • (Predicting what they could raise as an objection, so only say if necessary.) If I need to, I will sign a contract that commits me to stay with the company, and, if I decide to leave, I have to pay back that year's fees in full.	• In order to do the course part-time, there are ten tutorial days which I need to attend. In all, with study and learning days, it will take around 30 days a year for four years (including weekends and evenings) and I am only looking for ten days. • (To say only if required.) As a compromise, I am happy, if necessary, to take half of the days as holiday, however would like the company to afford me five days' leave.

An example of 'what's in it for the company/boss' justification for an MBA.

So, you have understood how to approach the boss and acted accordingly. You have also prepared your case for an improved package, understanding what you want and how the company and/or the boss benefits. Now it's just a matter of doing it!

THE OPENING APPROACH

Face-to-face is often seen as the best way to approach sensitive and complex issues. With a pay increase, so much can be interpreted in the wrong way by email or letter (see Chapter 3). There is nothing better than positive and confident emotions that will help support your case.

Approach the meeting with positivity and politeness. Prepare an agenda of discussion and have it with you (perhaps even give a copy to the boss). Within the agenda, make sure you cover the subjects that you said you would when you first asked for the meeting.

Agenda for discussion	
• review of business and current role	Really enjoy role. Especially feel positively challenged by the two people I'm mentoring. Steve has had great start to the company and now runs one of our top five accounts – the client says he couldn't be happier with him. Barbara has fitted in well and has presented to the department new research, which will really go down well with clients. Include other information from 'ideal outcome' sheet (see page 168). Questions to ask: • What are your thoughts on the development of Barbara and Steve? • Are there any new accounts that we are currently pitching for? If yes, can I be of help?
• ideas	Suggestions: • Mentor system has been hugely successful, why not develop it and give every non-manager a mentor? • Weekly meeting to discuss each other's business, what works and what doesn't. Learn from each other's experiences.

• development	MBA info on 'ideal outcome'(see page 169). You could include development on the agenda even if you were going for a financial increase, as it is a key part in most career roles, and the money normally comes from a different budget. For example, if you were increasing your role as a mentor, perhaps a mentoring course.
• remuneration	From 'ideal outcome' sheet (see page 168).
• AOB (any other business)	

An example of an agenda and some notes attached
for your use.

When communicating justifications for an increase, it is probably better to ask your manager to consider a pay-rise and let them offer you the increase, rather than you proposing. If they ask you what you want, then, unless the meeting has highlighted any key issues that may affect this, (for example, redundancies), go with your ideal income.

When you want a specific addition to your package, e.g. the MBA, you need to make your proposal; otherwise you could be leaving them guessing what it is you actually want!

Most bosses realise that additions to packages and pay rises are a difficult and sometimes stressful subject to bring up, and it's highly likely that they have been through the same process themselves with a superior before. Remember to justify your proposal for a better package, telling them why you deserve it, as well as what they will gain from it. Remember that there is a fine line between arrogance and confidence, and what is important is to stay on the right side of it.

As you are asking for an increase or addition to your package, it is likely they will give you feedback on your performance.

If it's not given, you may want to ask for it, as an understanding of how you are doing, as well as discussing areas of development, often helps. It can be positive to use this as a platform to ask questions about the direction of the department and company as well as about your boss's own role. Having a genuine discussion and showing interest in them and the company can help to build your relationship with the boss, as well as allowing them to get to know you better. I always say that when people know you, trust you and like you, you are well on your way to building a strong relationship – assuming, of course, you feel the same way about them!

A PAY NEGOTIATION WHEN YOU ARE OFFERED A NEW JOB

A cautionary note

This, in theory, is easier than when you are in an existing role, as you have managed to impress your prospective boss very recently, enough to be offered the job. However, before we begin to talk about the negotiation side, consider the need for the job on offer. For example, if you are currently out of work and have no real form of income, you need to assess whether haggling over a few extra pounds a day, compared with accepting the offer, makes you vulnerable to someone else being given the job. If income is less important at the moment than getting the right job and conditions, as you have several offers and some savings, then fair enough, but this is one to be careful with, as, unlike negotiating for an MP3 player, there can sometimes be no turning back.

Perhaps the best time to negotiate is when you are already in a job, especially if you are relatively happy in the current role, as your alternative to taking the new job is still acceptable to you.

Let's assume you have balanced the pros and cons of the new job and are currently with another company, but are keen to move **if** the conditions are right. The position has been offered to you, but you want to improve the package.

If you intend to negotiate, under no circumstances accept the role there and then, as your negotiation possibilities have pretty much gone. Politely thank them for the offer and say that you would like to seriously consider it and will get back to them (I would also tell them when), and seek agreement that this is OK. Be prepared for them to ask why as well, and have a positive and honest answer to this, for example:

> *'I really appreciate the opportunity and need to give it some serious thought. I would like just a couple of days to do this.'*

Most employers will agree to this, as they understand that changing jobs is a big decision, and it's important to be happy with the right location and package. If pushed, you may want to say this.

Comparing the differences in role

Now that you have some time to think, look at the differences in the role on offer compared with your current responsibilities. Also include any market knowledge information that you can find out: for example, average wages or other additional benefits that are normally included. Speak to your network of friends/colleagues to see what you can find out. Having been for an interview, it's likely you would have done some preparation in order to get the job. Can any of this help you to determine the value of the role you have been offered?

Current job Accountant – small firm £36,000 9 – 5 20 minutes from home	**New role additions** Senior accountant as opposed to accountant Dealing with larger clients (c.£80 million as opposed to £5 million turnover)
New job offer Senior accountant – large corporation £40,000 Company pension Additional three days' holiday Company car. 9 – 5.30 50 minutes from home	Mentoring two new accountants Evening entertaining More travel (domestic) Client knowledge suggest wages c£45,000 for this company

Looking at the additional responsibilities of the job offer compared with your previous role.

Begin with the end result in mind

As with the package negotiation earlier in this chapter, have three outcomes in mind: ideal (your opening offer that you feel would be good for you, but justifiable to the new company); good (an improvement on their offer and enough to move happily from your existing employer); and acceptable (if they do not offer at least this, then I am prepared to stay where I am).

Current offer: £40,000 Company pension Additional three days' holiday Company car 9 – 5.30 50 minutes from home	New role additions Senior accountant as opposed to accountant Dealing with larger clients (c£80 million as opposed to £5 million turnover) Mentoring two new accountants Evening entertaining More travel (domestic) Client knowledge suggest wages c.£45,000 for this company	
Acceptable £44,500 pension, holidays, no car	Good £44,500 pension, holidays, car	Ideal £46,000 pension, holidays, car

Your three outcomes.

The conversation

Now you have the information to hand, choose your way of communicating it – face-to-face, by phone, letter or email. A face-to-face meeting allows you to read body language, which may give away emotions that expose signals of intention to be flexible in package offers (for more information read Chapter 3).

An example conversation could include a 'wage sandwich' that has considered your outcomes with the additional responsibilities in mind.

'Hi John, it's Simone here. Thank you for offering me the job, and I have given it some serious consideration. Whilst I would love to come and work for McHenry Associates, I need the package to reflect the move I am

making. The role you are offering involves more travelling to work, around an extra hour a day, and whilst I am very happy to do this to gain a role with your company, the additional cost is around £1,000 per year. Also the move to you involves significant responsibilities that I know I am more than capable of, including mentoring two new employees and looking after your top accounts worth in excess of £80 million. If you would increase your offer to £46,000, then I would be happy to start with you in a month's time and prove to you I am worth the investment.'

The above example is justifying the increase and not backing yourself into a corner, because what you are **not** saying is that you won't consider other offers; you are merely saying what **you** want. From this John can say, 'yes', 'no' or make you a counter-offer, and then you have a choice as to what to do. If a counter-offer is made, remember to consider your good and walk-away outcomes and use the 'if and then' approach. For example, if John offers you £44,500 with the other conditions, you can either accept it, or if you feel the money side is exhausted, perhaps there might be something small that may be of use. For example:

'OK John, I understand that £44,500 is the best you can offer, and if you allow me to start in seven weeks' time, then I am happy to accept the role and look forward to starting on September 4.'

In this instance, you have always wanted to go away for a three-week break with the children, and, in normal working circumstances you couldn't take that amount of time off. This is the perfect opportunity to get this if the company can afford for you to start a little bit later. I took such an opportunity when my first son was born. I was poached by a company that I really wanted to work for. Having negotiated the financial element to my package to what I felt was the maximum, I realised that there was something else that would be very valuable to me at this stage in my life, and that was to spend extended time with my wife and new-born baby. I said that I would happily agree to take the job if I could start in ten weeks' time, and they agreed. This allowed me to have valuable father-son bonding (although the constant nappy changes did put a bit of a downer on it!), and that was something money couldn't buy.

Or, if they mention that in addition to your current job, a car is an attractive part of the package, you may want to trade that (assuming the car is not hugely important to you) for an increase in money.

> '*I appreciate that a car adds a significant amount to the package, probably around £15,000 over 3 years. However the financial element of the package is more important to me. If I was to not take the car, then would you increase the offer to £46,000?*'

Importantly, this does not back the potential future employers into a corner as it is merely a suggestion, and therefore if they say no, or offer a compromise solution, then you have the choice as to whether to accept the offer or not.

The idea is to always keep the door open for as long as possible, and leave you with the choice of whether to accept what's on the table at that point or not.

IN SUMMARY

1. Prepare your case for an improved package. Look at internal and external resources. Make your justifications, and importantly consider what's in it for the company/boss.

2. Understand how best to approach your boss and at what time. Profiling and preparation may help.

3. Have three outcomes in mind: ideal, good and walk-away.

4. If you are not going to accept the final offer, make sure you have a good alternative.

12
Creating the life balance you want

Have you ever wondered what it would be like to adjust your working week to suit your life's needs?

How would you like to:

- Start and finish work early so that you can pick up your children from school?

- Have your lunch-break at 11.30 so that you can go to your spin class on a Wednesday?

- Leave at 3 pm in July and August so that you can enjoy a long weekend during the summer?

- Work a three-day week, allowing you time for you, your family and friends?

A couple of decades ago, if you had suggested some of these, people would have looked at you as if you were a deluded fool. However, as life balance becomes increasingly important and companies begin to realise that to keep their best employees they have to try to accommodate the needs of the individual, the idea of either flexible or part-time hours has become more of a reality.

It is still an area to address with considerable preparation, as employers need to see the intrinsic benefits to them of changing the system. You also have to be clearheaded about both the up- and the down-sides of altering the amount of work you do, or the way you work. However, once you have decided you want to go for a change, the important thing is to come up with solutions rather than problems, as if an employer can see the value to both you and the company, they are much more likely to agree to your proposition.

This chapter does not debate the complex issue of what's legally required, as this is likely to change over time, with governments and pressure groups continuing to push for more quality of life for families, couples and individuals. Procedure and etiquette need to be considered, and these matters are well covered in specialist brochures and websites, or they can be discussed with dedicated advisers – they will not be covered in this book. Nor do I take into consideration what employers can or cannot say to you as these are also things that are governed by legislation that can change (and indeed just because they can't say it, it doesn't mean they are not thinking it). Nor is it designed to lead you to believe that there is a fool-proof system for success in persuading employers of the merits of giving you what you want, because quite frankly there isn't. This chapter is designed to allow you to think effectively about how to create the life balance you want.

What you do have to do is make sure that your relationship with your boss is at its best when you approach them to talk about flexible hours. Good communication has proved to be a key element to successful companies, and for a boss to agree to a change in working hours often takes time, effort, trust and faith. Bear this in mind when you decide upon the time-frame you set yourself to 'communicate' your wish to work more flexibly.

DOWN TO BUSINESS

There are two areas that we will discuss. Firstly, flexible hours: adjusting the timings of your working day to suit both your own and your company's needs, while working the same number of hours over a year; secondly, changing from full-time to part-time.

The examples set out in this chapter all involve families and children. This does not necessarily have to be the case: details and working terms can be adapted to suit anyone wishing to benefit from part-time or flexible hours.

FLEXIBLE HOURS

It is really important to think of approaching flexible hours from two perspectives: your own and your employer's. Firstly, you need to know what you want to achieve: a late start, an early finish or perhaps leaving two hours early in the summer. Let's assume that you want to start at 7.30 am and finish at 3.30 pm; and, as a second example, we will use an early finish in the summer with the same details.

Look at the company you work for and its make-up, the type of work it does, whether it already adopts a flexible-hours system or employs part-time staff (both the business as a whole and your department). Detail anything that gives you a feel for what may be possible and any areas that you can show (within the knowledge you have of the firm) where flexible hours could improve the working of the company.

How to pay less for more

Company name	AN Other Retail Limited – suppliers of fashion across Europe
Employees	350 approximately, including full-time, part-time and job-share.
My department	Accounts, employing twelve full-time staff and one part-time, including Director, two managers and ten Executives. Of the thirteen, six have children (including me); Steve (the Director), his children are 7 and 10; Amy (my manager), her children are 3 and 5; Steve and Claire have one each, their children are 12 and 14 respectively; Deborah (part-time) has a baby aged 8 months.
My position	Executive working in a team of five (including one manager, one part-time). Been with company for three years (second-longest Executive).
My working hours	9 – 5 with 1 hour lunch-break (taken at 1 pm). All of the department work these hours and have the same lunch break.
My role	Liaising with 50 clients across five countries – UK (20), France (11), Germany (7), Spain (6), Cyprus (6). Get in at 9 am and return voicemail calls left from first thing in the morning (approximately eight). Peak time seems to be 9 am until 3 pm (many during lunchtime, although UK lunches are between 1 – 2 pm, non-UK lunches tend to start at 11am/12 pm GMT).
Useful information	We are number one supplier in UK, France and Germany, number four in Spain and Cyprus. Fashion retail is a highly competitive market and relies heavily on customer service. Business is fluid throughout the year, but busier around January/February, May and June and September and October.

External information	Rival companies are mixed in their use of flexible hours. Company A, C and E allow flexible working and have excellent staff retention, whilst B and D don't.

Having a detailed understanding of both your company and department allows you to judge better the feasibility of your request, and also perhaps to glean some useful ideas of how you can show the benefits to your employer of your flexible working.

AN EARLIER START TIME

In this case, you want to finish earlier than the allotted time to enable you to pick your children up from school in the afternoons and do the household chores, allowing leisure time at the weekend to dedicate to the family. This you need to balance with the needs of the company.

I am happy to work the same number of hours per day, but would like to start and finish earlier, in order to pick my children up from school

The company wants to increase its productivity and be the number one fashion retailer across Europe.

Matching the information you have about what the company wants with what you want, you can begin to put a justifiable case together.

LOOKING AT IT FROM THEIR PERSPECTIVE

List the benefits that you see the company will gain from you changing your working hours to suit your daily routine. Examples could be:

1. The time difference is generally one hour ahead for France, Spain, Germany, and two hours ahead in Cyprus. I will be available from 7.30 am GMT/BST (8.30 am in three of the countries and 9.30 am in one – all local time); this will give them valuable additional customer service, rather than having to wait for someone to return their voicemail. At the moment Cyprus does not have any cover until 11 am (local time) and the other European countries 10 am – well into their working day.

2. Providing extra customer service may help to improve the company's position in Spain and Cyprus, and maintain or strengthen France and Germany.

3. Working between 7.30 am and 9.00 am will allow me to be more productive, as there will be no day-to-day distractions with people, and I will be on my own in the department.

4. I can help with other team members' European accounts at this time – my colleagues will be safe in the knowledge that their clients are being looked after. This will help to give the office a feel that it's open nine and a half hours a day as opposed to eight. Equally, there may be someone who wants to start and finish late, therefore increasing the opening hours further, potentially allowing us to branch out to the USA (which is between five and eight hours behind).

5. I will feel more motivated as an employee, as my personal needs have been taken into consideration by my employer.

6. I will still be in the office for the peak hours (9 am – 3 pm).

7. My lunch break will be 1.5 hours earlier and will allow me to cover the office (fielding calls, etc.) when everyone else is at lunch.

Once you have listed all the benefits, think of any potential reservations that your employer may have about your request (whether they air them or not is neither here nor there, as the important thing is to answer any underlying thoughts that may stop you from getting the flexible hours). Examples are as follows:

1. If you get flexible hours, we would have to rethink the structure of the department, as others will potentially want them too.

2. It complicates matters too much.

3. There is no-one here to open the office that early in the morning, and we have sensitive information in here.

4. Who will cover your calls between 3.30 pm and 5.00 pm?

Alongside these objections, think of your answers. In cases where you feel that the reservations are what your employer is probably thinking but hasn't actually said, you need to consider whether to include solutions within your conversation. Potential answers could be:

1. If other people did want similar opportunities, perhaps a system could be considered that allows for this: some working late, some working early (note, it's looking at it from **their** perspective, i.e. not saying some starting late and some leaving early). To the clients, this will look as if we have increased our operation from an eight-hour day to an 11-hour day, listening to the needs of our European partners and potentially expanding to the USA. I am more than happy to work on a rota to allow this, if required.

2. It's a simple and effective method of getting more out of a day. There will be one and a half hours' extra cover, and more work will get done (with me working smarter and faster during the periods when the office is quiet, i.e. during other lunch breaks and the period before 9 am).

3. I am more than happy to take on the responsibility of opening the office in the morning.

4. I will inform my clients of an alternative contact for the late afternoon period. But it is worth bearing in mind that that is a quiet time. Over the last month I have analysed the incoming calls: we come into the office with about 35 voicemails from European partners; the vast majority of calls (over 160), were between 9 am and 3 pm, when I will be in the office; the calls between 3 pm and 5 pm reduce to around 20. It is also worth noting that I will be covering other people's calls from 7.30 am. I am also more than happy to move my lunch-break so it doesn't clash with everyone else's. By doing this, I can deal with clients' requests that have previously been left on voicemail for people when they return from lunch.

Now you have all the benefits and answers to potential objections, it is time to pick an appropriate time to approach your employer, ensuring you have followed the correct procedure.

LEAVING TWO HOURS EARLY IN JULY AND AUGUST

A tangible reason for this may help: in this instance, it's the summer holidays and you would like to spend more time with the children.

I want to work the same amount of hours over the year, but re-distribute the time so I spend more quality time with my children during their main summer holiday.

The company wants to increase its productivity and be the number one fashion retailer across Europe.

Calculate the amount of time that you want from the company in that period. In this case, assume it's 90 hours over two months (nine weeks at ten hours per week – leaving work at 3 pm every day during July and August). Therefore this time needs to be made up elsewhere. You need to show that the re-distributed 90 hours will be beneficial to the company/department.

The benefits that the company gain from being flexible, in this instance, could include:

1. During peak periods (Jan/Feb, May/June, Sep/Oct – 24 weeks) I am happy to work until 5.45 pm (a total of an additional 90 hours). This will enable the office to be open a further 45 minutes during peak periods, allowing for fielding calls, invoices to be sent out on time and payments chased.

2. Providing that extra customer service (extended office hours) puts us in line with our competitors, many of whom are open until 6 pm.

3. Working between 5 and 5.45 pm will allow me to be more productive. There will be no day-to-day distractions with people as I will be on my own in the department, enabling me to field calls and complete any paperwork.

4. I can help with other team members' accounts at this time, allowing individuals to go home at 5 pm safe in the knowledge that their clients will be looked after for a further 45 minutes during the peak period.

5. I will feel more motivated as an employee, as my personal needs are being considered alongside the working requirements.

Again, think of objections that may arise and possible solutions. Some could be similar to the ones above, but there could potentially be others as well. For example:

1. If we allow you to finish early in the summer, then everyone will want it.

   Possibly this is true. Perhaps you could offer it to the others as well, and, if it proves popular then we could create a rota that allows up to five people to leave early for those weeks. The volume of business is more than 25% down during the summer. Having people covering the office in the peak months until 5.45 pm will benefit the business, with more traffic during this time.

2. But what if it doesn't work?

   Then trial it and we review it after the first year.

NEGOTIATION IS A TWO-WAY THING

It may be that the boss is happy to agree with your requests if you present them well, showing the benefits they will receive.

But in some cases, there may be the need to compromise in order to get some of what you want: for example, three early finishes instead of five. In which case, if you are happy to do this, then your calculations of times reduce accordingly.

A compromise could be offered, or an objection to your request may be given. But an objection does not necessarily mean no to any type of flexible working. Always listen out for signals that **may** indicate an alternative could be an option.

LISTENING FOR WHAT IS NOT SAID

Often what is not said is as important as what is actually said. For example, if when asking for earlier start times, an answer comes back:

> 'No, 3.00 pm is too early to finish work because calls do come through between 3 and 3.30 pm.'

What this is not saying is that 'only a 5 pm finish is acceptable.' Perhaps 3.30 pm may be OK, as this has been brought up as a reason for not allowing 3.00 pm. Consider asking;

> 'What time is acceptable?'

Or

> 'Is 3.30 pm acceptable?'

WORKING PART-TIME

As with flexible hours, it's important that you look at a proposal to work part-time from two perspectives: your own and the company's/department's. In doing this, you are likely to examine it in a way that takes into account their potential reservations about the idea (if any) and also look at ways in which part-time hours can genuinely work for both parties.

There is no point in listing the personal benefits of changing from full-time to part-time work, as I am sure anyone reading this chapter has already done this in massive detail already! However, it is worth understanding how important changing to part-time is to you, and considering alternatives you may have if the employer says no.

As an example, you are a salesperson who wants to go from a five-day week to a three-day week. In this case, you ideally want a three-day week, although if needed, you would accept a four-day week. You have just returned from maternity leave and have a daughter, Emily, who is now 9 months old, and you want to spend more time with her. Your motivation to work is still high, and you enjoy your job (and the independence and 'adult company'), but don't want to continue full-time.

As with flexible hours, look at the company as a whole and your own department, detailing its function. Does it currently embrace part-time hours? If not, is there potential for it to do so? Could it benefit from part-time staff? Do your competitors offer such benefits? If so, how successful are they? If they are successful, what makes it work effectively?

Look at your specific role; an overview version is given opposite. In order to help you understand the concept, I have kept the description brief, but when you do it for your own role, you will need to put more detail here. Alongside the role, put your ideal and acceptable (if you are prepared to have an alternative) outcomes with an idea of your solution (based on knowledge of your department and its business).

Potential questions to ask yourself include:

Desire	Solution searching
Working a three/four day week.	1. Can the job be successfully covered in three/four days? If so, can you prove it?
	2. Are there any other employees/ex-employees willing to job share?
	3. Do you know of any friends, or friends of friends, who may be interested (and adequately qualified for the role)?
	4. If the company required you to work more than your initial proposal, would you (and the employer) be happy for you to work from home for some of the time? Can you show that working from home would work?

Current job 35-hour week Mon – Fri Senior Sales Executive in a team with four other executives and a manager.	The role would be difficult to fulfil in its entirety in a 3-day week. AN Other company successfully adopts a system that has workers job sharing (similar role to mine).	Ideal solution Job share with someone who wants to do a two-day week.
Detail your role here. Specifically in relation to responsibilities and workloads (your CV should help here).		Acceptable solution Reduce key accounts to 12 (previously 16 on a full week) and work a four-day week.

A version of a job description with two part-time solutions.

Ideal solution – job share with someone who wants to do two days per week
- Five-day-a-week cover. Lucy, an ex-employee, left to have a baby, would like to come back to work on a part-time basis. She could job-share with me. Between the two of us, we will cover the full working week.
- Lucy knows the business, so needs no induction and can hit the ground running, saving time and resources.
- Accounts have permanent representation, reaping the benefits of two minds on their business, and having full cover every working day. All accounts will be informed of share and know which days we work.
- Happy, loyal and motivated members of the team.

Acceptable solution – a four-day week, downsizing key accounts to 12
- Four-day-a-week cover, giving a financial saving to the company.
- Choice of day off would be Friday, statistically the day when least business is converted. Though am flexible with day if company would prefer an alternative.
- Allows opportunity for individuals within the team to take on more responsibility and rise to the challenge by taking on the other four key accounts.
- A happy, loyal and motivated member of the team.

The ideal and acceptable solutions, with the benefits to the employer.

As with flexible working, remember to think of possible objections that your employer could have – and their solutions.

ALTERNATIVES TO STANDARD FLEXI- OR PART-TIME

Below are a couple of other ideas and questions to ask yourself when preparing your case for creating the life balance you want.

Desire	Solution searching
Working term-time only.	1. Can the job be covered during these times, either by permanent or temporary staff (at no additional cost to the employer – apart from the money they save from your salary)? In certain sectors, especially in retail outlets, some of the more junior roles can be covered by students in school holiday periods.
	2. Is the work you do not time sensitive? Can it be covered when you return (potentially agreeing to additional hours the rest of the year)?
	If having all holiday periods off is out of the question, will working one/two days a week fewer in the school holiday times be of benefit to you? Can this also work for the employer? Can you prove it?

Desire	Solution searching
Changing your lunch-break time to suit your lifestyle (For example, to attend a gym class)	1. Are there calls/opportunities missed because of the current lunch hour? Sit at your desk for a few lunch-breaks, and document opportunities missed and the benefits of having cover at this time.
	2. If you were to have your lunch-break at a different time, how would this affect the work? If it was negative, what could you do/put in place to positively change this? If it's positive – give them proof!
	3. Can you prove that the change of time of your lunch-break will increase (or certainly maintain) your current output. Can this be specifically attributed to the change in hours?

THE BENEFITS TO EMPLOYER AND EMPLOYEE

In a lot of companies, flexible hours and part-time working have led to positive outcomes for the employer as well as the employee, and many case studies have been written as testimony to this. Listed below are a few benefits that can be seen for both sides. The list is still growing. Getting the system right can often take time, flexibility and patience; but ultimately if an employer can keep their highly trained, most effective employees, and employ new and fresh ones as the company grows, surely it's worth the effort!

Potential benefits to the employer	Potential benefits to the employee
Focused and loyal employee	Highly motivated and happy fitting work into life (rather than the other way around)
Retain best of staff	Feeling of being valued and listened to
Reduced absenteeism	Healthier employee
Increased productivity	Happier employee
Greater talent wishing to join the company	

IN SUMMARY

1. Decide what it is you really want and a reason as to why you want it. For example, to start and finish late so as to take your children to school, or work a three-day week to enable you to spend more time

194

with your children and fit in all other elements of life.

2. What are your company's/department's goals? Can your new working proposal help achieve them? If so, how?

3. Look at your company as a whole. Does it offer flexible hours already? Does it employ part-time staff? Is it working successfully? Have you examples of other companies successfully operating flexi- or part-time within your industry?

4. Look at your specific department and examine it as you did in point 3.

5. Examine your role within the department. Can it be done as effectively (or more effectively) with your proposal of flexible/part-time hours? If so, how?

6. List the benefits the department and/or company get from your proposal.

7. Think of the objections that may come up and have good solutions.

Last but not least …

13
It doesn't
end there ...

Well, if you've gone through this book from start to finish, you will now understand the concepts of negotiation. Or, with your increased salary, you may already have bought a new house (and sold your old one), taken ownership of a new car and revived your kitchen with several new electrical goods, including a rather flash DAB radio, whilst negotiating with the local stately home a great price for your wedding reception.

If so, then this book has succeeded in its intentions!

In this final chapter, I am going to do a quick re-cap, including looking at other areas of consumer life where negotiation is possible, explore the world of car-boot sales (where you can be both buyer and seller), and – finally – show how your negotiation skills can have uses even beyond the worlds of money and work.

I KNOW YOU MUST BE TIRED OF HEARING IT, BUT ...

If I had to choose just three elements to remember when you negotiate, they would be: preparation, preparation and preparation. If you prepare effectively, your chances of gaining a better price are significantly increased (as are your chances of finding out which product or package you really want). Preparation affects all elements of the negotiation from start to finish. Create your own preparation sheet that will help you complete a successful negotiation, one that can evolve as you become more competent and learn new ideas. Opposite is an example of one that will help get you on your way.

THE LIST IS ENDLESS

Earlier in the book, I went into detail about specific areas of buying and selling where negotiation could save you thousands of pounds. But those were simply a few of the possibilities. Here are some additional areas where negotiation can take place:

- 2nd-hand cars
- **internet/phone packages**
- **kitchens and bathrooms**
- **gym packages**
- garden furniture and electricals
- courses and memberships
- spa days/treatments

- clothing
- extensions
- household furniture
- insurances
- advertising
- nanny fees
- antiques

For the examples highlighted in bold, I am going to go on and give a little bit more detail. This will not be exhaustive: if you have read the rest of the book, you will already be an expert negotiator!

Kitchens and bathrooms

1. Consider what you want doing. Is it your kitchen **and** your bathroom (if so, see point 2)? Is there a particular style? Is there a store that can offer the electrical goods that go with

A negotiator's preparation sheet

Product(s) (list the type of product you want, not including brand):

....

Benefits to negotiating/preparing: 1. .... 2. ....

Max time spent preparing: ....

Research (list specifics):   Internet ☐   Television ☐
Brochure/prospectus ☐   Newspapers ☐   Shops ☐
Special offers ☐   Magazines ☐   Other ☐

Product requirements:	must-haves	nice-to-haves
	....	....
	....	....
	....	....
	....	....
	....	....

Top three choices and their benefits:

1	2	3
....	....	....
....	....	....
....	....	....
....	....	....

Package (including stores/locations to purchase from):
1. ....
2. ....
3. ....

Ideal	Good	Walk-away
....	....	....
....	....	....

My approach when negotiating will be (e.g. polite, knowledgeable and confident):
....

Approach (salient points that will help me achieve my ideal outcome – e.g. sales points/questions)
1. ....
2. ....
3. ....
4. ....
5. ....
6. ....
7. ....

Observations learnt from the negotiation ....

the units (in which case definitely read point 2!)? Is it units and tiling?

2. If you are in the process of renovating both, and are considering companies that sell both, then make sure you read the packaging part of Chapter 9 and use this to good effect.

3. Research the companies. Get the brochures, visit the stores, speak to the salespeople and ask the questions you need answers to. This is the browsing stage: get quotes for what you want (in writing). Consider your must-haves and nice-to-haves and whittle your list down to perhaps three.

4. Think of your three outcomes: ideal, good and walk-away.

5. Negotiate with choice 3 and then 2, being careful not to promise them the business, however impressing upon them the need for their best offer as it really will increase their likelihood of getting your custom. Use your research to good effect with the salesperson, comparing, for example, qualities of tiles and their relative pricing, or the design of the units and your preferences compared with budgetary constraints, always leaving the impression that you can be swayed. Use the package offered by choice 3 as leverage if you think it may help. Get choice 2 to a position where you would be happy to accept it, if choice 1 was not to offer at least your walk-away rate.

Internet/phone package

1. Research the relevant packages on offer. Work out what else is important to you over and above price. Is it service, free weekend calls, add-ons, speed of internet, modem included, free installation, etc? Beware of hidden extras –

it is important to clarify what's **not** included in the price as well as what is.

2. Short-list your options to three.

3. Negotiate with options 2 and 3 for a better price, before tackling your first choice.

4. Use the information that you have gleaned about each company and the prices/packages you have now got to negotiate a better deal. For example, if Company A offers £22.99 per month to include broadband and evening and weekend calls for free, whilst Company B has the same package for 19.99, but does not have the service standards that you want, highlight the £3 difference as being very important to persuade Company A to reduce their price. Talk about it as being £36 a year. If they say: 'It's only £3 more a month', you can of course turn that around and politely say: 'You're right, so why don't we just deduct it?'

Gym packages

Look at your options. Get the various prices of gyms. Make sure you are comparing like-for-like (e.g. all off-peak, or towels included).

List the must-haves compared with nice-to-haves, and prioritise your options.

Negotiate with your third choice first, being careful not to guarantee them the business. Use your knowledge of the gym market to good effect, e.g: when Gym C claim that Gym A is more expensive, talk about Gym A's larger swimming pool and Pilates class times that suit you better; however, price is also relevant and if they give you a good enough incentive, then you could be persuaded (use your own wording here). Make sure they know they have a real chance of gaining your business, if they give you a really competitive price.

Go through a similar process with Gym B and use the latest package offering that you have negotiated from Gym C as leverage.

When you finally get to choice A, you have already got a good alternative sorted if you don't manage to persuade them to do a deal that is right for you.

ENJOY THE FUN OF CAR BOOT SALES

A car boot sale allows you the unique position of being able to buy and sell at the same time. It gives you the opportunity to develop the skills that we have spoken about throughout this book: preparation, questioning, listening, body language, rapport, bargaining and closing – as well as developing a strong understanding of how strategy can help.

It enables you to look after your pennies, when brand new doesn't necessarily matter, and it's more about getting the product you want at a great price. Furthermore, it can de-clutter your house and make you some extra cash at the same time.

And for most of us, there are few excuses, as you don't have to travel too far to find one!

This section is split into two – buying and selling. It is worth reading both: as I have always said in negotiation, it is good to see things from the other person's perspective, as you are much more likely to strike a deal if you look at it from both sides.

You as seller

Invariably, you are getting up at the crack of dawn to load your car full of the junk ... er ... quality goods that are now surplus to requirements, which you feel someone else could benefit from.

Below are a few pointers to help the sale go well and also to make it enjoyable.

a. Choose the best car boot location for your products. Look at the local paper, search on the internet and ask your friends about their experiences.

b. Think about what you want to achieve. Are you wanting to get rid of clutter at all costs, for example making sure you come home with everything sold? If so, perhaps prepare a big, colourful sign that you can take out of your car for that final burst, and prepare to shout out your best sales lines (maybe use a microphone if the coordinators of the event allow it).

Are there items that you will only let go of for a certain price? If so, then have a crib sheet of minimum prices with you.

c. If you are unsure of the market value of your products, perhaps look at some internet auction sites or second-hand shops for advice. Also, have a quick walk round the boot sale and see what your competitors are offering (assuming you have someone watching your stall).

d. Use your negotiation skills to best effect and don't put price tags on the products – this also saves you time.

e. If possible, choose a prominent pitch that you feel will have high traffic (lots of people passing by), and if it's wet, avoid the muddier and wetter areas.

f. Use the day's weather to your advantage. If it's hot and sunny, put your barbecue and summer shirts in a prominent position, and if it's wet and wintry, lead with the waterproof jacket and galoshes.

Think of investing in some drinks – the more time people spend in front of your stall the better! Even if they are not buying, the interest that will be created by other people seeing queues in front of your stall will entice them over to see what's so great about your products. Equally, when you get a thirst …

g. Arrange your items in a logical format and use space effectively – think of how the best shops lay out their stores (believe you me, a lot of detailed thought goes into this). For example, men's and women's clothes separated and sorted into sections. When you've arranged it, go to the other side of the counter and see what it looks like from the buyer's perspective.

h. Remember what retailers do (and this book talks about): package things up, offer three for two, BOGOF (Buy One Get One Free). Everything's a WIGIG at a boot sale (When It's Gone It's Gone).

i. Bring lots of change and somewhere safe to store the cash.

j. Be vigilant. Again, use the stores analogy: most good shops have security scanning for thieves. Where possible, make sure there are at least two of you.

k. Remember to read at least Chapters 2 and 3 to give you valuable insights into how to get the best out of your sale.

You as buyer

a. See all the selling tips above and look at them from the

point of view of a buyer. For example, with reference to point h above, why not ask: 'If I buy both these products, will you sell them to me for £10?' Also, with reference to point c, if you know what you want to buy, research the product before you go and see what price you can get it for elsewhere.

b. Get there early to buy the best products, and if you're prepared to chance it, stay until the end to snap up the bargains. Make sure you have a good look round before you buy, as you never know, the item you desire may be on sale in several locations, and you can play one off against the other.

c. Bring plenty of bags to carry your treasures away in.

d. Don't assume that the sellers will be as astute as you (they may not have read this book!); they may not have laid out their table well and the real goodies could be hidden under the garish jumper that they used to wear in the 80s.

e. Look out for dents and marks: if they don't adversely affect your decision to buy, that's fine, but you need to point them out in order to gain a better price.

Whether you are a buyer or a seller, you can use your new found skills to make the day enjoyable and also profitable. Presentation and thinking about what would attract customers (you are one yourself, remember) will allow you to maximise your sales. Making a proposal and using your understanding of body language will help you get the best value from the car boot sale. However, preparation, bargaining, communication and understanding the market will help in both cases.

Of course, the one product I hope you don't see at a car boot sale is a copy of this book. But I'm sure if it is there, it will be well thumbed, and the owner won't allow you to flick through its pages before purchasing!

PERSONAL RELATIONSHIPS

Some of you, seeing the heading for this section, might think: 'Oh no, he's not going to tell us how to be salespeople in order to attract someone, is he? How tacky!' Relax. I certainly do not advocate selling oneself to partners, as I have seen this in action, and it is often distasteful. However, what **can** be useful in helping to sustain a long-term relationship is learning how to resolve differences through listening, questioning and compromise – a distant relative of negotiation, but a softer and more acceptable route.

An example where compromise is useful: you might want to go camping in Spain for your holiday, while your partner might prefer a luxury hotel in Italy.

Is there a compromise to be had?

What is it you really want from a holiday (must-haves)? Is it Spain? Is it camping? Is it an activity holiday? Or is it a sense of adventure? What's important to you?

What would be nice, but not necessarily a must (nice-to-have)? Is it Spain? Is it camping? Are outdoor activities important? Is it because you want to be by the sea or in the mountains?

What is it your partner really wants (ask questions and listen to the answers)? Is it a holiday in Italy? Is the idea of having a luxury hotel important to them? Are they wanting to be pampered or rested?

What is it they would like, but is not vital? Is it Italy? Or is it the luxury 5-star hotel? How about a spa nearby?

Match each other's must-haves and see how many nice-to-haves you can both incorporate.

A simple approach, perhaps, but so often a successful one – a win-win outcome is the best solution for all.

THE BEST NEGOTIATORS OF THEM ALL – TACKLE ONLY WHEN AN EXPERT!

When I am about to embark upon this type of negotiation, I need to psych myself up beforehand. The steps I will often take are:

1. Look at myself in the mirror and ensure I have a positive and confident posture.

2. Stare at myself, repeating several times (until I believe it) 'I am a better negotiator than they are, I am a better negotiator than they are.'

3. Walk with purpose down the stairs and towards the front room. Before I enter, I take a deep breath, then stride into the room and exclaim: 'Now boys, it's time for homework!'

Children are amongst the best negotiators – why is this? Because they haven't yet been suppressed by the beliefs of many adults that negotiation is embarrassing: they still have the confidence to ask for more than what's on offer and not to be content with their lot.

I allow my children (within reason) to negotiate on certain things – and say very clearly when they can't.

For example, my children hate homework but love computer

games, and this has often proved a valuable negotiation tool to 'persuade' them to do their studies!

This is where the 'if and then' technique has come in handy:

> *'If you complete that page of maths and get at least eight out of ten, then I will allow you to play your favourite game for 30 minutes on the computer.'*

Notice that alongside 'if and then' are some very specific parameters: eight out of ten needs to be achieved, and **then** you can spend 30 minutes on the computer. You may also want to consider starting by telling them they can spend only 20 minutes on the computer, knowing full well they will demand 40, and you can settle on 30 – thereby sharpening your negotiation skills as well as theirs!

SUMMING UP

I hope that this book has given you the confidence to negotiate and improve your lifestyle – giving you more money to either spend or save; and in the case of those who want to improve their life balance, a few insights into how to approach the boss and create the time that you want. Also, I hope you have found this book as enjoyable to read as I have to write.

Negotiation can be for everyone, and once you get into the pattern of asking for money off, the process becomes a natural one, and, before you know it, you are wandering into a store expecting to pay less than the asking price.

But it's much more than that: negotiation is a skill that is highly transferable to many of life's challenges.

To highlight just a few:

1. It teaches you not to accept the norm, to be confident to ask for what you want, and to do it in a way that is acceptable to other people, be it at work, with friends or at home.

2. It helps you to plan strategies for what you want to achieve – beginning always with the end result in mind and working your way towards your goal, with logical and good preparation.

3. Negotiation's softer skills, involving reading people, gaining rapport and communicating effectively, will help you to develop friendships and business partners, as they grow in knowing, trusting and liking you.

Happy negotiating!

Glossary

Although these are often terms used for a wide variety of subjects, I have made them specific to negotiation.

Assumptive close – This is when you close a deal assuming that your terms will be met. For example 'I look forward to receiving your £35 cheque in compensation' or 'So that's £420 including delivery', when delivery hasn't been mentioned before.

BATNA – stands for Best Alternative to a Negotiated Agreement – when you ensure you have an alternative product you are happy to purchase if the seller will not agree to your walk-away rate.

Buying signals – when someone gives away that they are keen to buy. Sometimes people do this unconsciously. For example, when buying a property, they plan how they are going to change the room in front of the sellers: 'We could pull up the carpet and put wooden flooring down, and then put Stephen's toy-box in the corner over there.'

Conditional offer – an offer based on certain conditions. For example, 'I will offer you £200 if you include a pack of ten blank CDs.'

Facilitate trade – someone who facilitates trade is a person who helps a deal happen.

Good rate – an outcome that you are happy to achieve.

Ideal rate – the best outcome you would hopefully achieve (normally your opening offer).

If and then – this is normally related to a conditional offer. It allows you to make an offer that is only relevant if they agree to your terms and in no way commits you otherwise. For example: '**If** you include the curtains and carpets, **then** I will pay £400,000 for the property.'

Managing expectations – making people understand the terms that you are happy to trade between. For example, telling a salesperson that you are able to spend up to £500 and no more.

Outcomes – your thoughts as to the possible end results of a negotiation, usually two or three. See ideal, good and walk-away rate.

Pre-close question – this is when you think the salesperson has agreed to your terms of contract, but to be sure you ask a question to confirm this. For example, you think they have agreed to your price, and you ask the question: 'Will you include gift wrapping for £100?' Whether the salesperson says yes or no, they have confirmed their agreement to the price unless they object to it at this stage.

Price sandwich – often used by a seller to hide the price between two benefits, thus softening the blow of a cheap rate! For example, when you are selling your house, you say: 'I am happy to complete the deal on 16th January at £495,000 and will include the curtains and carpets as well.'

USP – stands for Unique Selling Point. A unique selling point is what specific benefit a particular product has that is a unique proposition to the consumer.

214

Variable – a part of a deal that is not set in tablets of stone – a bargaining chip. For example, price can be a variable – how much you are willing to pay for a product; or a music CD could be a variable if you are buying a stereo system. It is often added value that may be 'nice' to have, but is not necessary for you to agree a deal.

Walk-away rate – a minimum rate or an outcome for you to agree a deal. If these terms are not met, you are prepared to walk away.

Win-win – a phrase that is used to describe the perfect deal (certainly in business). It's when both parties benefit well from the negotiation. In the case of consumer negotiation, you come out with a good deal and the retailer profits from selling the product.

Index